Think Digital

Act Digital

Speak Digital

Publisher's Note

Every possible effort has been made to ensure that the information contained in this book is accurate at the time of going to press, and the publishers and authors cannot accept responsibility for any errors or omissions, however caused. No responsibility for loss or damage occasioned to any person acting, or refraining from action, as a result of the material in this publication can be accepted by the editor, the publisher, or the author.

First edition published in the United Kingdom in 2023 by Ideas for Leaders Publishing, a business of IEDP Ideas for Leaders Ltd.

Apart from any fair dealing for the purposes of research or private study, or criticism or review, as permitted under the Copyright, Design and Patents Act 1988, this publication may only be reproduced, stored, or transmitted, in any form or by any means, with the prior permission in writing of the publishers. Enquiries concerning reproduction should be sent to the publishers at the following address:

Ideas for Leaders Publishing
42 Moray Place
Edinburgh
EH3 6BT
www.ideasforleaders.com
info@ideasforleaders.com

ISBN
978-1-915529-19-0 – Paperback
978-1-915529-20-6 – Ebook

Cover design: www.nickmortimer.co.uk
Typesetting: Sopho Tarkashvili

Acknowledgements

I would once again like to express my deep sense of gratitude to everyone in the long list of people who supported me along my DBA research journey, starting with my remarkable thesis supervisor, Professor Maurice, Thevenet and the leaders I interviewed during the research phase. The insights they gave me were priceless.

I would like to thank Professor Michel Kalika for his important encouragement and guidance in helping me publish this book and honouring me with its foreword, and Stephen Platt for his consistent support and advice throughout.

Thank you also to Roddy Millar and Ideas for Leaders for believing in the project that led to this book, with particular gratitude to Chris Murray for his skill and diligence in helping to summarize this shorter volume.

And again, my final heartfelt acknowledgement for the support and great love of my family to whom I dedicate this book: Monique, Julien, Jeremy, and Noemie, and my parents Kozhaya and Mona.

Contents

Foreword

By Michel Kalika

This book, *Think Digital, Act Digital, Speak Digital* by Jean Elia is a remarkable and useful piece of work in many respects.

Remarkable, firstly, because it is a logical sequel to his Doctorate in Business Administration (DBA) thesis at the Business Science Institute.

Remarkable, too, because his work addresses a highly topical issue – the digitalization of businesses – not in a simplistic way, but with a concern for rigour and from the ambitious angle of business transformation, which represents a veritable managerial and strategic challenge for the leaders of any organization.

Lastly, it is remarkable because his research is the fruit not only of a review of the literature but also, and above all, of a series of 21 in-depth interviews with bank CEOs.

This is why Jean Elia's book is useful for senior executives and managers.

It is **useful** because he writes with a concern for communication and the sharing of ideas.

It is also useful because of its conclusions, which clearly set out managerial recommendations that can be put into practice by company management teams.

Finally, it is useful because the book has been designed to create managerial impact in companies, which is the primary purpose of a DBA.

Jean Elia's book should be on the desk of every manager concerned about the digital transformation of their company.

Professor Michel Kalika
President, Business Science Institute
August, 2023

A Note from the Author

The goal of this book was two-fold:

1. to present my research on the theory and in-the-field practice of leading DT in the financial services industry
2. to use this research to create some practical guidelines for CEOs that they can use more successfully to plan and implement DT. These guidelines would cover many aspects of the process, including the role that leaders ought to play in the journey.

This book is intended for all senior executives and board members within the financial sector, be it in banking, insurance, asset management and fund industry, and all other related activities. Throughout the process, I received positive feedback from this community about my research; of particular interest was the information I was gathering on the practices and views of their peers.

For those wishing to access the academic references and detailed footnotes and gain a deeper insight into the methodology used, an extended version of the research is available from EMS Editions:

Leadership of Digital Transformation:
The case of CEOs in the banking industry

ISBN: 978-2-37687-881-0

For further information: https://www.editions-ems.fr/boutique/leadership-of-digital-transformation/

Chapter One

Introduction: Digital Technologies Are Transforming Banking – and the World

Digital technologies are transforming the world, and no industry or professional sector is immune. Upstart technology-driven players and highly digitized companies are disrupting traditional market practices and activities. To survive, incumbents must be ready to throw out or radically transform their business models. Uber's demolition of the historic taxi business model, or Netflix's successful assault on both video chains and cable television (and even the film industry, as proven by Netflix's industry-leading 36 Oscar nominations in 2021) can be replicated in any business sector or industry.

The financial sector in general and the banking sector in particular have seen their fair share of disruptive technology players invading the market, including FinTechs, that is, technology-focused start-ups launching innovative products and services, and neo-banks that make payment systems accessible through digital channels. No less than 26,000 FinTechs were operating worldwide in early 2021.

These new and potent competitors are already disrupting and dismantling the banking industry's value chain, but that is only the beginning. The business model of tomorrow's bank will be radically transformed. As shown in the figure below, the 'bank of the future' could include banking without bankers, operations without infrastructure, service without branches, payments without middlemen – just to mention a few of the realistic potential scenarios.

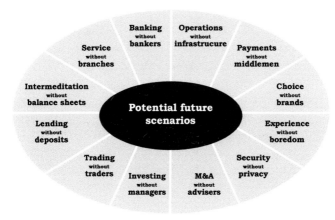

Figure 1.
Deloitte Potential Future Scenarios[1]

Put on notice, incumbents in the financial sector – no different from incumbents in all industries – are trying to react, but not always succeeding. A 2018 McKinsey study showed that while 80% of companies were investing heavily

---

[1] Deloitte, 2016 - https://www2.deloitte.com/us/en/pages/financial-services/articles/banking-industry-disrupter.html)

in digital transformation (DT), only a third were succeeding.

It is important to clearly define what we mean by digital transformation.

Digital transformation is the optimal use of new technologies, which transforms the way a company interacts with its customers, thus 'enchanting' the latter's experience; the way it functions internally, hence optimizing its efficiency and enhancing employee experience; and the way it disrupts the business model itself to create more value and enlarge the market base.

In this book, we examine the state of the banks' response to the industry's DT, focusing especially on leadership of DT. This book is built on the rigorous research and analysis I conducted for my Doctor of Business Administration (DBA) thesis for Business Science Institute and Université Jean Moulin (Lyon 3). This thesis, examining how banking leaders are leading DT, was based on insights and information of real banking DTs from interviews with a panel of bank CEOs, as well as an in-depth review of past academic studies on leadership, digital transformation, and a combination of both.

My professional experience, described below, put me in a unique position to conduct this research, analyze the results, and draw the implications that offer guidelines for successful DT.

My Personal Background

The early years of my almost 30-year career in the insurance industry included some IT functions (as I had studied IT and worked in IT before joining an insurance company) as well as sales and operations. As I rose through the ranks, leadership became an increasingly important focus of my job. For the past 16 years, I have been the CEO of three insurance companies, first in Egypt, then in Morocco, and finally in Luxembourg where I am the CEO of the insurance subsidiary of a large banking group. Thus, I developed throughout my career two passions: a passion for transformations and more specifically DTs, and a passion for leadership.

In reviewing the academic research on DT and leadership, I found extensive research on leadership as expected, less extensive but interesting research on DT (although some of it quite technical) and very little on the leadership of DT, perhaps because this combination is relatively new.

I thus decided to conduct research to identify and describe how banking leaders were conducting DTs in their companies.

My first goal was to develop an understanding of DT from the digital as well as from the transformational point of view. I wanted to explore how DT would impact the bank's interactions with stakeholders. That is, how it might shape the business models of banks. I also explored how DT might impact the organizational structure and management of the bank.

Finally, I wanted to develop a better understanding of leadership and its role in DT. Specifically, I would look at which leadership characteristics and styles would be best for change and for transformation in general and in particular for DT. The role of the leader in conducting DT is also central to this analysis. And finally, I wanted to explore how CEOs were coping with change and how they were 'living' the DT in their banks.

From all of this research, I hoped that the key factors that could help CEOs in leading DT in all its phases would emerge.

My career gave me several advantages for this research. The first is my experience leading DT as CEO of three companies. In all three positions, I was focused on helping my companies gain a competitive advantage through DT, despite resistance from many stakeholders, particularly in the wealth sector who, at the time, were convinced that digital technologies were not essential for this client segment.

The second advantage that I had in conducting this research was access to many CEOs in the banking sector thanks (or due) in particular to my international experience and the business model we operate in, what Business Science Institute president Michel Kalika refers to as "the opportunity of the environment".

My research was thus built on three sources of information.

The first source was an extensive review of academic research published in the fields of DT and of leadership. My goal was to liaise these two fields of research, leading to a better understanding of the *Leadership of Digital Transformation.*

My review of academic research related to DT allowed me to define DT from the digital (or technical) point of view and from the transformational (or substantive change) point of view. I also explored the impact of DT in the banking sector on

1. customer experience;
2. operational efficiency;
3. a transformed future business model; and
4. organizational structure, notably through Agile methods and Agile at Scale organizations.

For my review of the academic research on leadership, I focused on leadership theories in general, including leadership traits, styles, and contingency, as well as research on transformational leadership and leadership of change. I also reviewed, still in terms of styles, traits, and contingency, the limited recent research on leadership in the context of DT.

The second source of my research consisted of exploratory, semi-directive interviews I conducted with a significant number of banking CEOs. I made sure to have a contrasting sample of CEOs, working in different banking sectors and different countries, in order to get as much diverse feedback as possible. I was looking for real-life insight and perspective about their experiences in leading DTs in their banks, including their assessment of their personal role in conducting DT. This insight and feedback on their practices, difficulties, challenges, and success (or lack of), gave me important information through which to identify key success factors in leading DT, which helped me to later develop recommendations for banking CEOs.

In my analysis of the interviews, I focused on four areas:

1. How the CEOs defined DT and how they perceived the bank of tomorrow.
2. The CEO's journey to digital technology – a step-by-step review of the DT development and implementation process.
3. The impact of the DT on the organizational

structure in their banks, which could be quite substantive, and included, for more advanced banks, deploying 'Agile at Scale.'

4. The role CEOs played and their leadership in conducting DT.

My research then entered into a third phase in which I compared and contrasted the findings of the CEO panel interviews with the past research I had documented in the literature review and my own personal perspectives and experiences as a leader in the financial sector.

Throughout my research and analyses, I was guided by two academic approaches: *grounded theory* and *epistemological pragmatism.* The grounded theory approach emphasizes the importance of keeping the different parts of research independent of each other. This for me meant that when I interviewed the CEOs for my field research and analyzed the interviews, I was not influenced by any information or conclusions that might have emerged from my literary research or from any previous knowledge or experience I might have had. Likewise, my literature research and analysis were not influenced in any way by any information or conclusions that might have emerged from the interviews. The epistemological pragmatist approach calls for acquiring knowledge in order to address problematic topics or situations by rendering them understandable. The outcome should be pluralist proposals that resolve the problematic issues of the subject. In sum, I sought through these research approaches to remain completely objective and practical throughout the entire process.

Based on the information and insight into leading DT acquired through my field research and literature research and analyzed independently and then all together, seven themes emerged. These seven themes – which cover every facet of leading DT – are the basis for the following seven chapters of the book, with each chapter focused on one theme, as follows:

- **Chapter 2. The leader's understanding of Digital Transformation.** This chapter explains different CEO views on DT, including when to invest and what this investment should entail, and how different leaders define the DT experience. This chapter also explores leaders' views of the bank of tomorrow.

- **Chapter 3. The journey to Digital Transformation.** This chapter examines how leaders are putting in place a DT strategy, reviewing transformation plans, the duration required for DT, the optimal timing of launching the transformation, and other factors such as culture and communication. The chapter also offers a more detailed description of DT projects and initiatives that were deployed or being deployed at the banks in the panel, such as client platforms, workflow automation, and other technologies, including APIs (Application, Programming Interface), RPAs (Robotics Process Applications) and smartphone APPs.

- **Chapter 4. The impact of Digital Transformation on the organizational structure.** True transformation requires a full reorganization. Beyond structural changes, e.g., moving people around, DT requires a new mindset through which people are empowered and responsible, motivated to think disruptively and accept change. Most banks are implementing an Agile organization, partially or 'at scale'.

- **Chapter 5. The leader's role in Digital Transformation.** The leader's role in DT can be divided into three levels of involvement: the 'strategist' who creates the DT plan; the 'promoter' who can sell the transformation plan to stakeholders; and the 'owner/sponsor' who is personally involved in the execution of the strategy.

– **Chapter 6. The leader's traits for Digital Transformation.** Perhaps one of the most pivotal traits for leaders to succeed in DT is vision. An ambitious, optimistic, and innovative vision serves as the launching point of successful transformation. Leaders must also demonstrate the courage to challenge resistance and assume the risks of DT, as well the ability to learn about DT and to orchestrate its design and implementation.

– **Chapter 7. The leader's style for Digital Transformation.** The transformation of an organization is a collaborative effort, giving 'participative' leaders who are able to engage people in this effort an advantage. At the same time, a more 'directive' leader can add pace and intensity to the transformation, especially valuable for initiatives working on a shorter timeframe. Different leadership styles fit different situations.

– **Chapter 8. Overall leadership of Digital Transformation.** In the digital age, the mystique and the 'aura' of leaders are no longer effective nor possible. The most important success factor for leading DT is the ability to motivate and trust people. If fully engaged in the process, leaders will find that they are not only successful, but are also finding satisfaction and even fun in the work.

- In **Chapter 9,** I conclude with **a CEO's Guide for a Successful DT** based on five recommendations built on the insights developed in the seven themes.

Each of the chapters is divided into three main sections. The first is a thematic analysis of the interviews conducted with the CEOs. The second presents the findings that emerged from the analysis. The final section of each chapter is a discussion of these findings and recommendations.

The wide-scale disruptions caused by digital technologies, which bring both threats and opportunities, leave no room for error: organizations will inevitably be forced to launch or accelerate DT. In the following pages, you will discover, through the insights of on-the-ground bank CEOs leading DTs and my analysis and interpretation of their experiences, which issues to address, which mindsets to change, and which roles and approaches to take that will ensure sustainable success for your financial institution in the transformed world that lies ahead.

Chapter Two

Digital Transformation
As Seen By CEOs

The first theme of the research is the leader's understanding of digital transformation (DT) – that is, what leaders need to transform in terms of client experience, operational efficiency, the business model, and attention to people and jobs.

PART 1: ANALYSIS
HOW DO CEOS DEFINE DT?

The client experience refers to how clients live and feel their interactions with the bank. As one of the panellists explained, "Clients expect to have the same experience when buying a financial product from a bank as when buying a ticket, clothes, or any other product on the Internet." For the leaders in the panel, enhancing the client experience requires offering services that allow faster automated interactions with the bank anywhere, anytime, and on any device (a concept known as ATAWAD). These services would move clients from physical interactions, such as visiting a branch, to digital interactions, such as using the bank's mobile application.

DT also enhances the internal processes of the bank, leading to improved efficiency and increased productivity. Efficiency improves as processes are optimized and automated, eventually resulting in seamless Straight-Through Processing (STP). The productivity increase reflects the role that DT plays in improving the experience of employees (and other stakeholders from shareholder to regulators) just as it improves the customer experience. After all, employees expect DT to improve their own experiences as well as they provide enhanced services to their customers. As one CEO explained, "Employees cannot understand how we ask them to sell digital products that they cannot access themselves using the bank's tools."

What differentiates the CEOs' views on DT?

In my research, I found that the extent that DT will change the client relationship with the bank depended in part on the type of banking. For retail and corporate banking leaders in the panel, the emphasis was on real-time connectivity. One retail banker went further, saying that today's clients want technology to help them make decisions by giving them the ability to get comparisons, to get immediate responses to requests, and to access to the best prices available.

For private bankers, the human connection must never be severed, although they agree that low-added-value 'daily banking' can be covered digitally. However, banking functions related to 'key moments' in the value chain or even the clients' personal life must be handled by a real person.

Corporate bankers have the same approach as retail bankers, although the corporate banks in the panel tended to be more advanced in the DT journey.

According to the leaders in the panel, especially for retail and corporate bankers, the maximum level of digital technology and innovation should be used to fundamentally change the way a bank functions. Otherwise, DT would be little more than updated automation, improving the bank's capabilities. Instead, DT enables real-time connectivity with the client and is transforming the industry. "Digital transition is a complete change of speed, rapidity to access the information, connectivity, and interdependence between the client and the company," one CEO explains.

On the question whether DT is an enabler that complements and enhances current services, or a 'substitution' that completely takes over from the physical, most viewed DT as an enabler, not only enhancing current services but also offering new services. Some leaders did lean toward a 100% substitution – especially those leaders whose organizations were digitally advanced.

On the other hand, substitution did not mean 100% digital services and products, although some banks aspired to, and even had reached, the 100% threshold. For many of the bankers in the panel, some human-based services and products would always be available and necessary.

What and when to invest in DT?

Knowing what and when to invest in DT is a delicate balancing act. On the one hand, investing in digital can be very costly and – because these costs are rarely billable to the client and have to be fully supported by the bank – show a low return on under-investment, especially at the beginning of the transformation. However, the risks of not investing or under investing in digital are high since the consequence could be market value loss or even outright failure of the institution.

In general, therefore, investing decisions should be based on whether the investment
- generates more Net Banking Income for the bank
- reduces the costs of doing business
- reduces risks in general and operational risks in particular
- answers regulatory requirements
- increases productivity and efficiency
- increases client satisfaction and enhances their experience

How do leaders define the experience?

"Customer experience should be the first beneficiary of DT, before the employee, before shareholders," said one CEO in the panel, capturing the consensus that improving and enhancing the customer's experience with the bank should be the first priority of DT. For some, it is the only priority. For these leaders, back-office and process improvements (see next section) are not a goals in themselves, but simply the by-product of building up the customer experience.

Other leaders note that customers were once happy with 'satisfactory' service – leading to the generic phrase of 'customer satisfaction.' With the possibilities of digital, however, customers have higher expectations. They want their experience to be 'enchanting' or 'delightful.'

HOW DO LEADERS VIEW THE BANK OF TOMORROW?

What impact will DT have on the way the bank will look in the future? Will physical branches and human interaction still exist, or will it be fully digital instead? Perhaps the bank of tomorrow will be a mix of both. As with other facets of DT, the response of the panellists to these questions were varied and wide-ranging. I first review their thoughts on the impact of DT on the bank business model, then explore in more detail their perspective on the terms "digital" and "transformation."

Impact of DT on the business model

In terms of the future business model, most leaders see the bank of the future as fully digital on much of the value chain, especially for retail banks. In private banking, clients expect human advice and guidance – although digital capabilities can relieve bankers of the more mundane or repetitive tasks, freeing them up for the human involvement their clients expect.

None of the leaders believe the new business models of GAFAs, FinTechs or Neo-Banks will make the classic bank disappear. Banking is too complex and too regulated, and the returns are too low, the panellists said. Any threat from these new players will be on certain elements of the banking value chain rather than on banking itself. Disintermediation and aggregating are two examples of how these new players could disrupt the value chain while avoiding regulatory and business complexity constraints.

One interesting note: Successful leaders of DT refer to their banks as 'companies'; leaders lagging behind in DT still use the term 'banks'.

What is Digital in DT?

I asked the panellists how they defined the word 'digital' in 'DT.' Answers ranged from the elimination of paper and manual operations to humans being replaced to some extent by Artificial Intelligence. A number of leaders answered by differentiating digital from IT. Digital included the arrival of the Internet and other technologies that opened new distribution channels and new interactions with clients, as evidenced by e-banking and mobile applications, for example. Another differentiating feature of digital is the "brutal" (to quote one CEO) pace of change.

Digital is also the storage and use of big data – enabling banks to better understand client behaviour and to generate business to an extent that was impossible before. Future strategies will involve aggregating, packaging, and ultimately selling data, according to one leader.

Process automation is not new but has been significantly enhanced in the digital age.

What is Transformation in DT?

I also asked the panellists to describe their understanding of the word 'transformation' in DT. Transformation is fundamentally about large, ongoing change that is significant enough to impact how the bank works and the way it is organized. The challenge of transformation is overcoming legacy systems – and the "legacy of people, clients, and staff", as one CEO explained. Starting from scratch would be significantly easier.

Transformation also requires a change of culture, one that is open to change, innovation, and agility. Digital and innovation even need to become part of the bank's values, a key element in the bank's brand. "When clients think about digital, we want our bank to be the first thing that comes to their mind," said one CEO.

The impact of DT on jobs

There is no way to sugar coat the impact of DT on jobs: people will lose their jobs. Some leaders regret that automation and DT are "by definition job killers", as one panellist put it. Other leaders say there is no cause to mourn. As one CEO explained, inefficiency is being replaced by efficiency, which helps everyone. Whatever one's feelings about the turmoil in jobs, all acknowledge that many branches will inevitably be shut down and branches that are open will have less people in them.

Optimistically, one can argue that while jobs are being lost, new jobs are being created in the banks themselves or in the ecosystems of the banks. These are more technical jobs, and employees in the old jobs may not be a good fit for the replacement jobs. However, banks have a duty to upskill their employees as much as possible, which will not only allow these employees to move to the newly created jobs, but also allow them to acquire new skills that, eventually, might help employees find jobs outside the bank.

Another optimistic perspective is that staff will have jobs with higher added value, as lower value jobs or tasks are taken over by machines. For example, a private banker will have more time to advise client – and to acquire knowledge to inform this advice – rather than filling out compliance forms.

PART 2: FINDINGS

Finding 1. DT transforms the relationship with the client, giving clients direct access to the bank wherever they are and at any time. The shop is never closed. Another attribute of DT is 'porosity'– that is, the bank's services insert themselves seamlessly into the customer's other digital experiences, such as booking a hotel room or buying a product online.

Finding 2. DT augments operational efficiency. Automated processes become Straight-Through Processes (STP) that decrease time to market for new products and services but, perhaps more importantly, enhance the employee experience with more stimulating work. And employees are clients also, thus experiencing the same "porosity" of digital experiences.

Finding 3. The optimal degree of transformation varies based on the type of bank. For retail banks and to some extent corporate bankers, the maximum digitalization possible is the goal. For private bankers, the human touch is a vital component of their offering. No matter the type of bank, however, all panellists recognize the difference between daily banking tasks that should be digitalized as much as possible and key moments in which the client needs, in addition, human advice and empathy.

Finding 4. DT is costly, requiring thoughtful consideration of how much to invest and where. The panellists agree on certain key criteria for making the decision to go forward, notably whether the DT is useful and scalable, and increases income, productivity, and efficiency while reducing risks. There is no consensus on whether DT is a *complement* to or a *substitute* of existing structures and processes – a choice that has a great impact on investment.

Finding 5. The bank of tomorrow will be digital to a large extent, according to the panellists.

Where humans don't bring added value, digital tools will take over. While aided by digital tools, people will, however, always have a place in the industry. Clients want the expertise, experience, and, critically, empathy that only humans can offer. Technology alone does not threaten banks, but new, technology-driven entrants such as FinTechs, GAFAs, and digital or neo banks can disrupt significant sections of the value chain. Future business models will be 100% digital, or 100% physical with high digital capabilities. For some, the goal is not to be banks with digital capabilities, but to be digital companies that offer banking services. Finally, 'transformation' is more important than 'digital' in the concept of DT, with legacy systems (and people, whether client or staff) a major challenge.

Finding 6. The impact on people, and more specifically on their jobs, is on the minds of the panellists, some viewing DT as a job killer, others focusing on the added-value jobs that are created. All agree upskilling employees is an important component for any successful DT.

PART 3: DISCUSSION AND RECOMMENDATIONS

It is clear that banks want to interact with clients digitally anywhere and at any time, transforming the relationship in way that a branch closing at 5:30 pm cannot achieve. These interactions should be as smooth as other digital experiences, such as booking a hotel room or buying an item online. However, I believe banks should also think more deeply about the customer experience.

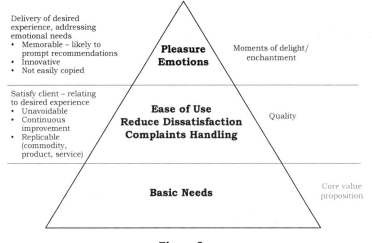

Figure 2.
The three levels of Client Experience.
Source: Body & Tallec, 2015

37

For example, the base of the three-level customer experience pyramid is *the satisfaction of basic needs,* manifested in quality products and services (see Figure 2 above). The second level of the pyramid, which was adapted by Laurence Body and Christophe Tallec from the work of Joseph Pine and James Gilmore, is *compliance with the company's commitment* – that is, customers feel that the company has fulfilled its promise to them. The third level of customer experience is *offering pleasure and emotions* – that is, the company delivers customer experiences that address the customer's emotional needs. While the CEOs in the panel spoke about the first two, the third level was rarely mentioned. Thus, I recommend that banks think about the customers experience in terms of generating pleasure and emotions rather than only enhancing customer interactions. Generating pleasure and emotions not only increases customer retention but also increases profits. Banks with sophisticated bank offerings need to make a special effort to *delight* their customers.

Digitalizing the front office and keeping operations manual is not good enough. The entire value chain should be automated, including back-office (aka core) systems. The resulting improved operational efficiency results in a more delightful experience for employees, increasing their motivation and commitment.

What needs to be digitalized? My recommendation: just about everything. As customer experience consultant John Goodman notes, whenever digital capability is available, clients prefer to use it. Yes, there are certain interactions at 'key moments' – developing a wealth management strategy or planning a succession – when human interaction and empathy are required. For all other banking activities, there should be no hesitation to digitalize whenever possible. And even for key moments, digital processes can support the banker.

When considering investment in DT, traditional constraints of budget availability and expected ROI may not be appropriate given the stakes for the future involved. In other words, investment decisions should be taken in the context of gaining an important competitive edge and setting ambitious goals. DT implies substituting what currently exists, which is costly at first but preferable to trying to maintain digital and physical activities and services. Substituting also requires diligence in investment choices: for example, do not invest in recruiting people for a process you are digitalizing.

The panellists do not see emerging models

of banking – e.g., open banking, digital banks, and platform banking – as existential threats. I agree in the short term, but believe a threat does exist, notably from FinTechs who can unbundle banking products, attacking portions of the bank's value chain. (See figure 3 below for examples of companies putting pressure on the life insurance value chain.) My recommendation: If you can't beat them, join them. Banks should pre-emptively partner with FinTechs and Neo-banks, becoming part of the new ecosystems being created. Explore platform banking. And better yet, see if you can beat them at their own game. Invest in incubators and acquire start-ups with the goal of creating your own ecosystem.

Whether one focuses on the job-cutting or job-creating aspect of DT, the fact is that all banks should invest in upskilling their employees. This is money well-spent, not only because retraining is always more cost-efficient than redundancy, but also because the effort will lead to a more engaged and motivated workforce employed in higher-value jobs.

Figure 3

Disintegration of the value chain- [Source: Berger-De Leon et al. 2016)]

The figure shows a value chain arrow with the following stages and associated companies:

Marketing & Product Development
- **Analytics:** eg Mu Sigma, Opera, Palantir, Tableau
- **Data:** eg Experian
- **Search Engines:** eg Google
- **P2P Networks:** eg CommunityLife

Asset Management
- **Third-party Capital Providers:** eg Blackrock, Bridgewater, Nephila

Risk & Underwriting
- **Specialists:** eg UIG
- **MGA (Managing General Agents):** eg Sureify
- **Risk Modelling:** eg RIMS, The Floow

Operations, IT & Support Functions
- **Insurance IT Specialists:** eg Actuaris, eBao Tech, Vertafore
- **Core Systems Providers:** eg Microsoft, Oracle, SAP

Distribution & Client Engagement
- **Affinity:** eg Tesco
- **Online Brokers:** eg Knip, GetSafe
- **Aggregators:** eg PolicyGenius, InsNext, CHECK24, Verivox
- **Fraud Analytics:** eg FICO, LexisNexis

Attackers   Supplier / Partner

'Disintegration of the value chain'

Chapter Three

Journey to Digital Transformation

The second theme of the research concerns *the journey to digital transformation*. This theme examines how to define a DT roadmap, how to make 'Digital' part of the culture, when to launch DT and how long should the process take, how to communicate during the transformation and to whom, and what major technologies need to be put in place.

PART 1: ANALYSIS
HOW LEADERS ARE PUTTING IN PLACE
A DT STRATEGY.

The journey to DT begins with the DT roadmaps put in place by the respective CEOs within their banks.

The Transformation Plan

The first step on the journey to DT is to pull together a digital strategy or "battle plan" for the bank. This strategy should be aspirational and ambitious, leading eventually to a whole new mission for the bank – either as a digital bank or as a digital firm proving banking services (and other services as well) – when the services are fully digitalized. At the heart of this new business model would be a transformed customer experience, as well as transformed operations that translate into a new employee experience as well.

In sum, the issues to be considered in drawing up the strategic plan include the following:

- **Purpose**: What, ultimately, is the bank's mission in the future, its eventual new 'purpose' or 'raison d'être' when fully, or quasi-fully, digitalized?

- **Business model**: In what type of business or activity does the bank engage? What services are added? Which current services are kept or abandoned?

- **Organization**: What role do the branches play in this digitalized business model? What are their competencies? What roles do individuals in the front and back offices play? How is the decision-making hierarchy structured?

- **Digitalization level:** Exactly to what degree will digital and automated services be offered? Will they replace or complement human activities?

- **Customer experience**: How is the relationship between the bank and the client transformed? What will the new customer experience look like?

- **Employee experience**: How is the employee experience transformed? How can the bank make the new roles and responsibilities of employees attractive to a talented workforce?

The Duration of a DT

The length of time for planning and executing the DT varied greatly among the panellists, ranging from 18 months to 5 years.

Whether the execution of the DT went according to plan depended on the timeframe chosen for the DT project. Some banks developed long-term plans that had to be adapted along the way in order to respond to changes and constraints that emerged, such as changes in technology, in regulations, and even, for some, in investment priorities.

In contrast, banks that had short-term plans – often 18 months – did not have to adapt their plans. Any changes in context or the environment in which the banks operated did not impact the plan to the point that required significant modifications or adaptations. In addition, with such short-term timeframes, banks were more focused on the execution of the plan than their counterparts engaged in longer-term plans. With a deadline looming before them, these banks were willing to accept an outcome that did not match the plan 100%. "Done is better than perfect" as far as they were concerned, adding that long-term plans would not be perfect either.

Perhaps a more apt description of the attitude of the short-term planners in the panel is the phrase, "*Launched* is better than perfect." That is, these banks did not wait till every facet of the DT was perfect. Instead, they launched the new platforms and tools, and then, incorporating their clients into the process, refined these DT elements through different iterations.

Another factor to consider in deciding on the timeframe of the transformation is balancing the time and energy spent on the DT with the time and energy required to keep running the business. By necessity, the organization cannot fully focus on running the business while also opening the bank to digital innovation. This dispersion of attention could lead to operational and client risks. At the very least, there will be some delays and errors – a general reduction in the perceived quality of services – that cannot be avoided. While loyal clients looking forward to the digital services on the horizon may be understanding for a while, their patience will run out if this transitional period goes on for too long – another reason a shorter-term plan is preferable.

The Timing of a DT

When is the best time to launch DT? Based on responses from the panel, there are a number of triggers. For some banks, it is a periodic review of corporate strategy, which includes a review of digital strategy. A gap analysis between a bank's present situation and its strategic goals for the future can accelerate plans for DT. Having a supportive Board of Directors and supportive shareholders – who must approve a DT initiative – can also be a factor in the timing. Other factors, such as new competitors or new regulations, can also indicate that the time has come to launch at DT initiative.

Culture

The panellists agree that banks must implement a digital culture to the point that digital becomes part of the bank's DNA. Every project, service, process, or product should include a digital approach. This digital omnipresence mindset is reflected in the words of one of the leaders: "If we cannot sell it online, we don't launch it." The inculturation of digital also requires that banks and their staff can interact in the new digital language with other parties involved, whether those parties are internal or external. Most banks in the panel have launched specialized training sessions and organized workshops and forums to ensure that their people understand the technology, as well as the new processes and ways of working required for DT.

Communication

For the majority of research participants, internal communication is another key factor in successful DT. Change will always induce fear, especially digital change that portends the takeover of human jobs by machines. The leaders believe that communication must consistently clarify the rationale and context of the transformation. Staff must understand and fully accept the reason DT is an important and positive advance for not only the bank, but specifically for them as well. "We need to 'own the story' to be able to communicate it better, so people could see there is a positive business case for the bank but also for them," explained one leader. External communication was seen as less vital to DT, with some believing that no external communication was necessary until the launch of digital products and services.

WHAT WERE THE PROJECTS AND INITIATIVES PUT IN PLACE?

Client Platforms

Perhaps the major objective for launching DT is the enhancement of the client experience. All of the banks in the panel have client platforms already in place, ranging from interactive websites through which clients can view their accounts to more sophisticated platforms that allow all client transactions and even, in the most advanced banks, online sales.

The priority is to connect digitally with the client, including for the most advanced banks through mobile services. Apart from a 100% digital retail bank, however, all the banks allowed clients to continue purchasing banking products through branches or bankers. For transactional banking, many of the banks will 'force' their clients to go digital, working hard at the same time to make the experience 'delightful' in the sense that customers have all the information they need in the best format possible.

Process and workflow automation

Digital client platforms required digitalizing back-office and front-office processes. "We cannot originate the product or the business in a digital way and continue its internal processing manually," explained one CEO.

In addition to upgrading and perhaps even changing completely the Core back-office system, the banks updated or created new systems for all of the major functions such as Finance, Accounting, Customer Relationship Management, Regulatory Reporting, and more. Digitalizing workflow information was also key. Linking the back-office processes seamlessly to front-office processes was essential. The banks found that processes that were not digitalized could block the entire chain and cause delays and operational risks.

Data

Data is an integral part of digital strategies. The exponential increase in data exchange over the Internet, however, leads to significantly increased risks of cyber security breaches. Data security is thus a major concern for all banks in the panel, leading to heavy investment on the protection of data. "You have to be very careful about data, values, and all client information and assets," said one CEO.

Along with data security, banks in the panel focused on data organization. Well-organized data can be more easily explored and mined for such activities as managing risks, making customer projections, and fulfilling regulatory reporting requirements – the latter especially dependent on organized data. Most leaders in the panel acknowledged that their data architecture is still far from optimal. They also lag behind in data analytics and data science for predictive analysis.

Other Technologies
The journey to DT required implementing new technologies, including:

- Robotic Process Application (RPAs), which allows robots to take over low-value, repetitive tasks.
- Smartphone Apps, foundational components for enhancing the customer experience.
- Application Programming Interface (APIs), which allows third parties to access the system, thus enabling systems to interact with each other. Only a few of the banks have implemented API, but 'APIzation' is on the horizon for the others.

External Partnerships
The APIzation trend reflects the belief by leaders that DT requires banks to engage with external partners, including FinTechs, through which they can develop, test, and try digital products and services. Some banks invested in FinTechs

– a win-win for the banks, who acquire FinTech technologies, and the FinTechs, who acquire (scrambled) data and an investor.

Finally, bigger banks invested in or launched their own incubators to host start-ups. FinTechs, start-ups, and other partnerships create the DT ecosystem essential for digitization.

PART 2: FINDINGS

Finding 1. The panellists emphasized the importance of beginning the DT journey with a clear strategy and detailed digital roadmap that takes into consideration the type of the bank's business and the bank's overall future mission. The roadmap would then describe the target organization, the target business model, the level of digitalization, the target client experience, and the target employee experience.

Finding 2. The period for implementing DT in the panel ranged from 18 months to 5 years. The shorter plans seemed to be more successful. Longer-term plans have been expensive and not always finalized. The challenge is to achieve the right balance between implementing DT and keeping the business running.

Finding 3. The timing for launching DT was important. Successful banks anticipate potential threats on their business models in the next 3 to

5 years to avoid finding themselves forced into change.

Finding 4. DT is not just another project; digitalization needs to become fully integrated into the bank's culture, so that it becomes part of its DNA.

Finding 5. An increase in communication – both internal and, to a lesser extent, external communication – is important to ensure buy-in by employees and other stakeholders.

Finding 6. DT projects are focused first on the client platforms. Digital client platforms require digitalizing core back-office systems and well as front-office systems, seamlessly linked together. With so much data come security risks, leading to heavy investment in security by the banks in the panel. They also focused on data organization, to ensure the best of the newly available data.

PART 3: DISCUSSION AND RECOMMENDATIONS

The panellists' view that developing a strategy is the first important step of DT aligns with past research on transformational leadership. Gerald Kane names strategy as one of four most important issues for DT, along with leadership, talent management, and organizational structure – noting that technology and its implementation is actually a small part of DT. In their *Guide for DT*, Emmanuel Vivier and Vincent Ducrey of the Paris-based HUB Institute write that leaders must define a clear strategy for DT, a real "battle plan" that must be explained to everyone in the organization to ensure buy-in.

The consensus in the transformation and leadership literature is that DT leadership should be top-down. I would agree. Many examples in the panel confirm that bottom-up approaches or attempting the transformation through a series of initiatives will not work. (See chapter five for further discussion on top-down DT leadership).

The DT strategy should cover three elements: the future customer experience, operational efficiency (which involves the employee experience), and the target business model. I believe the ultimate outcome of the strategy should be a new raison d'être, a new mission for the bank either as a digital bank or a digital firm providing banking services among other services.

It's important to decide on the ultimate target of the strategy and to develop a detailed roadmap for the entire journey from the outset. Launching small initiatives and reacting as you go is never recommended generally for strategic planning, and certainly not for a DT strategy. That is not to say that the plan is rigid. The DT strategy and its execution need to be agile and dynamic – continuously challenged and ready to make adjustments and changes in response. Using Design Thinking approaches, which involve empathizing, defining, ideating, prototyping, testing, and implementing, is one way to bake flexibility into the design and implementation of the strategy.

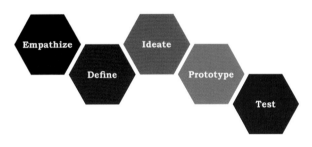

Figure 4.
Design Thinking Process.
(Source: Stanford d. School)]

Based on the examples concerning banks that are both part of this study and outside it, plus, of course, my personal experience, I suggest an optimal period of transformation of 18 to 24 months maximum. A shorter timeframe eliminates the need to adapt the DT plan to evolving stakeholders' needs, and allows the bank to take advantage of a short grace period during which customers are willing to endure a dip in the quality of services in anticipation of better services at the end of DT.

While there is no simple formula for when to launch DT, I recommend that DT be launched as early as possible. It is better to be proactive and anticipate potential threats to the business before they appear and require rushed planning and implementation.

Inculturation of DT into the organization is essential. The new DT culture of the bank can be summarized as follows:

Think Digital – digital is included in all processes and activities.

Act Digital – translate the thinking into action.

Speak Digital – interact digitally with all stakeholders, internal and external, who are present in the new digital ecosystem.

To successfully implement a DT culture, the culture must be *learning oriented* – that is, leaders and staff are in constant learning mode, which supports proactive anticipation and preparation for the future. In addition, top management buy-in is a critical success factor without which the cultural change required by DT will not occur.

Communication is essential to ensure buy-in and comprehension of both staff and clients. Internal and external communication must be handled differently, however. Internal communication must be continuous: the goal of internal communication is to accompany staff through every step of DT. External communication must be much more measured. Too much communication could make bank customers sceptical and could lead the bank to make promises it cannot keep. It would be 'digital washing'. I hence recommend communicating externally when milestones in the DT are reached, and to reassure customers periodically that services are being maintained during the transformation.

Finally, I believe that banks need to digitalize everything that can be digitalized, and ensure that digitalization projects are linked.

The technologies used and projects launched will not be the same for all banks, although some elements in DT are universal for all banks, starting with Data. For a successful DT, I recommend a large investment in Data, so banks can structure, protect, and share it via APIzation with the client and other stakeholders in the new DT ecosystem.

Technologies using Artificial Intelligence are highly recommended, from RPAs that can move redundant, low-value tasks from humans to machines, to the more sophisticated Machine Learning and Deep Learning, wich emulate (or tries to emulate) human thinking.

Chapter Four

Impact on Organizational Structure

In this chapter, I review *the impact of digital transformation on the organizational structure* – the third theme of the book. For most, but not all, leaders, the impact of DT on the organizational culture is considered significant. Leaders' opinions on the level of change required by DT differs. Unlike with other issues explored in this book, the different perspectives on reorganizing how banks function are not connected to the type of bank or the advancement of DT, but rather to the leaders' personal experiences, opinions, and background.

PART 1: ANALYSIS

THE ORGANIZATIONAL STRUCTURE

While some leaders in the panel believe no organizational structural change is necessary, the majority of leaders in the panel have already or are in the process of reviewing the organizational structure of their banks, ranging from consideration of small or moderate changes to potentially across-the-board changes. One proponent of a complete review explains his position: "To reach a successful DT you need to transform deeply the bank, and this goes through a global transformation of the organizational design". In contrast, some believe that only a partial review – perhaps limited to a department, a function, or even a process – is necessary.

The main goal of any structural review is to increase productivity and deliver projects more quickly. Another goal is to facilitate change by breaking down the barriers, including organizational silos and layers of management, that complicate staff involvement in any change initiative. With these barriers removed, staff will be more motivated to acquire a transformation mindset, contribute to change initiatives, and develop and put forward proposals.

The scope of the organizational restructuring depends on the leaders' assessment of what changes will lead to increased productivity and the faster delivery of projects. Fluidity and responsiveness are key, which is why most leaders disagree with two panellists who recommend a complete matrix organization restructuring. A matrix organization, these sceptical leaders argue, lacks a clearly hierarchical structure, which leaves no clear path for employees to navigate. The result is lack of employee commitment and late projects delivery.

At the heart of the restructuring challenge is the people of the organization. For some leaders, changing the structure means changing the people, especially on top teams. Any change will engender resistance, and change as extensive as DT – which requires adapting not only to new technologies but also to new managerial systems – will undoubtedly spark some pushback. New people who are not tied to the past are essential to the success of DT, these leaders believe. DT is a disruption and must be approached as such. DT projects should be viewed as blank sheets of paper: Start with the objective of the project, then figure out how to get there, including which people are needed (irrespective of which people are already in the organization). Even leaders who don't believe a complete restructuring of the organization is necessary acknowledge that DT will change the old ways of working, with more delegation, empowerment, and, consequently, accountability. "The idea is to make them product owners or mini-CEOs of their team," explains one CEO. However, not all people can handle the new responsibility and accountability, leading to high turnover, especially during the early stages of the process.

Agile and Agility
In reviewing their organizational structure, many leaders have chosen to incorporate, either

partially or 'at scale', the concepts and principles of Agility and the Agile Organization.

Agile started as a software development methodology in which the development occurs incrementally, as described by Ian Sommerville in his book, *Software Engineering*. The increments are small and made available to customers every two or three weeks, who are invited to give their feedback to the new systems – and to share with the software developers changing requirements. Speed and flexibility are key. For example, Agile reduces documentation by foregoing formal meetings with documentation in favour of informal communications.

As declared in the Agile Manifesto, Agile values "individuals and interactions over processes and tools; working software over comprehensive documentation; customer collaboration over contract negotiation; and responding to change over following a plan."

The Agile development method was created in response to the more traditional 'Waterfall' software development method, which, as its name suggest, one step cascades into the next. The five stages of Waterfall-based software development – requirements analysis and definition; system and software design; implementation and unit testing; integration and system testing; and operation and maintenance – is planned out from the beginning.

The incremental and interactive approach to software development quickly evolved into an entire Agile philosophy, now manifested in Agile management and the Agile Organization (see Figure 5 below). Stephen Denning described the five major shifts required for organizations to adopt Agile management:

1. *The goal of the organization is to add value for and delight the customer, as opposed to a goal of maximizing financial metrics.*

2. *The work is done by self-organizing teams as opposed to individuals reporting to bosses.*

3. *The work is coordinated by Agile methods with iterative work cycles and direct feedback from customers as opposed to bureaucracies with rules, plans, and reporting to higher ups.*

4. *The predominant values are transparency and continuous improvement as opposed to efficiency and predictability.*

Communication occurs in interactive conversations as opposed to one-way, top-down commands.

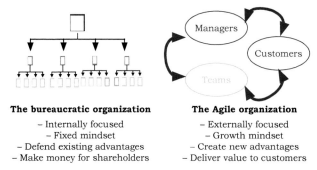

The bureaucratic organization
  – Internally focused
  – Fixed mindset
 – Defend existing advantages
– Make money for shareholders

The Agile organization
  – Externally focused
  – Growth mindset
  – Create new advantages
 – Deliver value to customers

Figure 5.
Bureaucratic vs Agile Organization[1].

Leaders who are adapting Agile at Scale – that is, reviewing a large portion of the organization through the perspective of the Agile approach – believe Agility is essential to the success of DT. Others emphasize the mindset of Agility over the methodology; this mindset, they argue, lays the groundwork for the delegation and empowerment of staff required by DT.

Not all leaders in the panel are convinced. As one sceptical leader told us: "Agile is overdone. People standing next to each other does not make it more efficient."

---

[1] Taken from *The Age* of Agile by Stephen Denning. Copyright© 2018 by Stephen Denning. Used by permission of HarperCollins Leadership, a division of HarperCollins Focus, LLC. https://www. harpercollinsfocus.com)

Meanwhile, promoters of Agile use Agile Teams to align the organizational structure to the customer journey – for example, by organizing Agile Teams by product or project, or for delivery or execution (see Figure 6 below). One CEO proposes agile teams that are dedicated to the customer journey itself, covering several products. Agile Organizations are also not necessary for every department. One bank established three criteria for deciding whether to incorporate Agile in a department: the link with the client, the speed and scope of IT developments, and the return on investment.

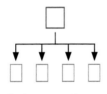

The bureaucratic team
– Top down
– Individual responsibilities
– Defend existing advantages
– Little interaction

The Agile team
– Autonomous
– Cross-functional
– Much interaction

Figure 6.
Bureaucratic vs Agile Teams.[2]

Agile should not be put in place for every project either. Some important structural projects, need to adopt a classic Waterfall approach, because

[2] Copyright: Stephen Denning, *The Age of Agile, as above*

the risks at stake are very high or the project requirements are very specific as with regulatory projects.

Examples from the panel of organizational structure changes

Here are few selected examples of how banks in the panel restructured their organization in response to DT.

- A retail bank restructured its branches, replacing universal branches with all services available to specialized branches divided by segment and value proposition. Although the bank is focused on decentralization and empowerment of the branches, no Agile at Scale is planned.

- A retail bank applied Agile Organizations in the delivery departments. Thus, tech people work together in small teams with customer journey experts, and people from marketing with the front office.

- A universal bank deployed "Agile Teams" who use conception, design, and incubation methods, test prototypes with customers, and rapidly deliver solutions. The bank intends to deploy Agile at Scale within two years.

- A private bank's successful DT changed the way people work; however, the CEO did not see a need to change the organizational structure.

- A big retail bank transformed its operational model, changing the way teams work together within the bank. IT and business work together with the Agile Methodology.

Agile at Scale at Komerčni Banka

The case study of a major Czech Republic bank offers clear lessons in the deployment of "Agile at Scale" reorganization. Komerčni Banka, a universal bank that provides a wide range of services in retail, corporate, and investment banking, serves more than 1.6 million clients and employs 8,000 people. For Jan Juchelka, Chairman of the Management Board and CEO, the technical part of DT was inevitable. The organizational impact of DT needed to be addressed, however, to ensure the bank would be responsive and proactive, and able to absorb the technological and other innovations that were coming.

The first priority was people – or more specifically, the relationship among people created by silos inside the organization. The bank focused on three silos at headquarters: Central Marketing, Central Software Development, and Central Project Management. The interactions among these silos were based on an internal client/internal supplier dynamic. People didn't work together; they either worked for someone or had someone working for them. Komerčni cancelled this structure, knocking down the silos and replacing them with squads (small 10-member teams) and tribes (groups of squads). The squads had no boss; they organized themselves around something to be delivered to an external client. The tribe had a single leader, the first level of management encountered in the new structure, who reported to a member of the Management Board. The tribe leader, in charge of up to 150 people, took the place of seven levels of management under the old structure. Eventually, the bank created 16 tribes and five centres of expertise. A total of 1500 people were impacted by the reorganization (all offered jobs) and 360 jobs were lost.

For Juchelka, several factors played an important role in the successful transformation. First, top management was deeply convinced of the value of the transformation. Second, the methodology was clearly understood by the bank's leaders. Third, a sustained effort was made to communicate with employees and beyond them to regulators, stakeholders, clients, and other stakeholders – all of whom needed to match or attempt to match the leaders' understanding of the methodology.

Juchelka also offers several guiding principles for a successful Agility and DT Journey:

- It's all about people and culture.
- Dare to jump into the unknown, let go, and learn.
- Focus on customer needs.
- Work together in cross-functional teams with a shared purpose and resource allocation.
- Minimize time-to-market, make quick decisions, test ideas in practice, and develop autonomy.
- Improve productivity, and reduce handovers and bureaucratic layers.

PART 2: FINDINGS

Findings on the impact of DT on the organizational structure:

Finding 1. Most leaders are reviewing or have reviewed their organizational structure as part of the DT process. There is no consensus on which organizational structure will most effectively support and deliver on the promise of DT. For some, reshuffling people is all that is needed. Most, however, are implementing the Agile organization either partially, focusing for instance on specific departments or value chains, or 'at scale' restructuring large parts of the organization into squads and tribes. All acknowledge the challenge of not beginning with a blank slate.

Finding 2. The structure must be uncomplicated, fluid, and responsive. Experiments with ambiguous and complex matrix organizations have proven problematic. Empowered and responsible people, motivated to think disruptively and accept change, are the linchpin of DT success. Silos need to be taken down so that people work together for the benefit of the external client, rather than working for each other – the internal client mindset.

Finding 3. For many banks, Agile methods for software development and projects leading to DT accelerates project delivery. For some, however, more traditional Waterfall methods are effective for updating legacy systems or for regulatory or structural projects.

PART 3: DISCUSSION AND RECOMMENDATIONS

Whether to reorganize the structure of your company and to what extent is a fundamental question. I strongly recommend a full reorganization based on an Agile Organizational Structure. The Agile Organizational Structure, however, should be deployed gradually, testing it in a small department first before scaling it.

This approach – a full reorganization deployed gradually – has a number of advantages:

- A full restructuring involves breaking down the silos in the company. As these silos are broken down and the internal client system disappears, everyone or nearly everyone is assigned to new roles.
- With a full reorganization, there is no place to hide. Employees who do not support or do not feel engaged in DT will probably leave on their own accord.
- Having everyone impacted by the

reorganization will reduce or eliminate feelings of injustice.

• New assignments and missions could motivate employees.

Timing is important. The planned reorganization should better occur before or at the beginning of the journey.

Agile extends beyond structure to incorporate mindset and culture. An agile culture is manifested through breaking down silos to foster internal cooperation and improved efficiency; eliminating internal clients to orient banks toward external clients; and, most importantly, empowering people and giving them responsibility. This agile culture and mindset are known as Agile Management. I recommend that Agile Management be deployed across the organization, developing the agile mindset that ensures employees are contributors to change and disruptors, rather than disrupted.

Although different software development methodologies for Agile have different strengths and weaknesses, I recommend Agile Methods, an incremental method built on relationships and interactions among people rather than top-down command. Sometimes, however, the Waterfall Model, in which actions are taken sequentially, is preferable. The Waterfall Model is arguably more effective, for example, for regulatory projects that have to meet 100% of pre-set requirements.

In a nutshell, I recommend Agile on three layers/levels: Agile methodology for software development, when applicable, Agile mindset or Agility for the management of the bank, and ideally Agile at Scale for the organizational structure.

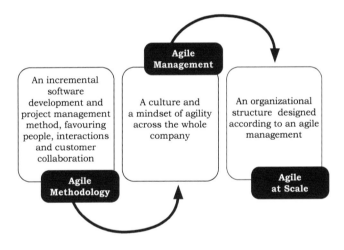

Figure 7.
Agile and Agility at three levels: methodology, management, and organizational structure (Source: Jean Elia)

Chapter Five

The Leader's Role in Conducting DT

The leader's role in digital transformation is the fourth theme of the book.

PART 1: ANALYSIS

THE THREE MAJOR DT ROLES FOR LEADERS

Leaders have a significant personal role to play in DT, from defining and implementing the strategy to ensuring an organizational structure and culture that supports the transformation. In many ways, the success or failure of DT depends in large part on the leader. In this chapter, I examine the three ways for leaders to be involved in DT: as Strategists, as Promoters, and as Owners.

Setting up the DT Strategy

As the DT Strategist, the leader must develop a strategy based on a long-term vision of the bank's business model – one that anticipates and pre-empts the disruption from new players and trends. The bank, the panellists agree, must strive to be the disruptors, not the ones being disrupted.

The leader must also ensure that DT is at the top of the bank's strategic priorities and that all digital innovations address the challenges of the bank: improving client experience and sales, reducing costs, increasing efficiency, and managing risk.

With resources scarce, leaders must take a holistic approach to implementing the strategy, allocating resources carefully among different initiatives with the above goals in mind, according to the panellists. To ensure the best allocation of resources, the leaders suggest first building a business case based on trends and opportunities. Naturally, not all investment decisions will work.

Promoting DT

Promotion of DT is more than communication. Leaders need to lead by example and show that DT is *everyone's* concern throughout the organization. If they are to make a compelling case for DT, they need to be convinced themselves that DT is essential – without this strong conviction, their promotion efforts will fall flat.

When promoting a change as extensive as DT, leaders must have a *story* to tell – a story that explains the why and the what of the transformation: why it is necessary and what it means to the employees – which is especially important given, as some panellists note, the very real risk of job loss. Transparency and honesty are vital in the storytelling.

Promoting a transformation is more than persuading employees to back a course of action;

they must be ready to adopt a new mindset of innovation, a mindset that lays the groundwork for a new innovation-driven culture in the organization. "The most complicated aspect of DT is to change people and their mindset to make it in line with the new world," explains one CEO. Communication and training are important to develop this new mindset, but even more importantly, the leader must embody the mission of transformation and develop a strong culture, the panellists say. Speaking to innovators outside the company – from millennials to start-ups to FinTechs – about what they are doing or inventing will help CEOs embody the spirit of DT. They should also speak with and support internal innovators and 'intrapreneurs' and invest in their internal start-ups.

Sponsorship and Ownership of DT Programmes

Sponsors or Owners of DT are the leaders most implicated in the transformation. They consider leading DT to be an integral part of their jobs. As one of the panellists explained: "Although I'm the CEO, or because I'm the CEO, that very specific digital change programme, I took it on myself." In other words, DT leadership is not a responsibility delegable to a Chief Digital Officer, for example.

The successful DT leaders in the panel want

to be close to the action – to the execution and to the field. Being close not only enables leaders to make more informed decisions, but also enables them to re-think and adjust the execution of DT in response to new developments. Some of the CEOs in the panel see themselves as militants on a mission to create agility and accelerate delivery. The continued presence of the leader also helps maintain the focus of the organization on DT.

At the other end of the scale are the leaders who are either not involved, or who keep their distance once they established the strategy. "I would get much more involved," said one CEO who acknowledged his bank's DT initiative was lagging behind. This CEO had managed DT as he had managed other transformations and changes in the past – an approach he now sees as a mistake.

In the panel, many CEOs were sponsors/ owners, some were promoters, and some were strategists only and not directly involved in the transformation. I noticed a correlation between the level of involvement and the level of DT advancement (see Figure 8 below). That is, DT was well advanced in the banks of directly involved sponsors/owners, engaged and even well engaged, but not advanced, in the banks with promoters, and in the early stages in the banks with strategists. It is clear, at least among this sample, that the more implicated the CEO, the greater the advance in DT. Although involvement is not a guarantee. Indeed, some banks with owner/sponsor CEOs were not advanced in their DT.

**CEOs involvement vs
Digital Transformation advancement**

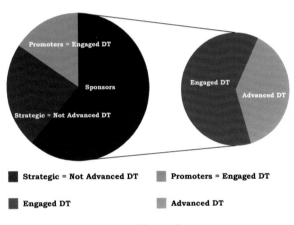

Figure 8.
Observed link between CEOs' involvement and
advancement of DT Source: Jean Elia

This chart is indicative and not exact; it reveals the pattern and link between the role that leaders play in DT and its progress.

Two other issues emerged from the research and the interviews with the panellists. The first concerned the extent of the leaders' knowledge about digital technologies. How much knowledge is required? A nuance emerged from the interviews with the CEOs: the difference between digital technologies and digital capabilities. Understanding digital capabilities – what digital does and can do – is essential for a leader to make informed decisions and understand trends. Mastering digital technologies – e.g., learning how to code or structure data – can be left to the digital technicians.

The second issue is the fun factor. I found from the panellists that the more they were implicated in DT and the more DT was advanced in their banks, the more fun they were having. When describing DT, these leaders would use words such as 'beautiful', 'challenging', 'exciting', 'positive', 'magnificent' and just plain 'fun.' I talk more about the fun part of leadership in chapter 8.

PART 2: SUMMARY OF FINDINGS

There were three levels of leadership involvement identified:

Finding 1. The Strategist defined a holistic approach to DT, managing investments and resource allocation for useful and profitably innovations throughout the organization. The strategy is based on the long-term vision of the CEO about the future of the bank and its business model, and can be changed if necessary.

Finding 2. The Promoter is convinced about the importance of DT and develops a story to explain the reason for the extensive change and how it might change to accommodate developments. The goal is to incorporate DT in the bank's culture.

Finding 3. The Owner/Sponsor is directly and personally involved in the execution of the strategy. There is no limit to this involvement.

The first three findings are cumulative. The leader needs to develop the strategy, then promote the change, and finally take ownership of the implementation.

Finding 4. Leaders should have a thorough understanding of the capabilities of digital. They do not need to master the technologies (e.g., programming codes).

Finding 5. Leaders should be having fun with DT – and will be if they are fully implicated in the transformation.

PART 3: DISCUSSION AND RECOMMENDATIONS

Vivier and Ducrey of the HUB Institute compared DT leaders to "generals" who, they write, "define the strategy but also decide on when to launch the assault." In a global executive study and research conducted by MIT Sloan Management Review and Capgemini Consulting, Michael Fitzgerald and his colleagues argued that DT could not occur without top-down leadership – although they emphasized the importance of communicating a shared vision.

As noted in chapter 3, DT strategies need to be top-down: bottom-up approaches will not be successful with transformation this extensive.

It's also important that a DT strategy be built on and incorporates the vision of the leader into a digital roadmap. "It's your vision, your vision, your vision, as a leader," notes one of the CEOs in our panel.

The DT strategy should also incorporate the leader's digital *ambition* for the bank. Allocating available resources is not enough. Leaders should challenge the resources available – that is, convince shareholders to invest more resources on DT or find a way to optimize existing investments to free up resources that can be shifted to DT.

I would thus recommend that leaders set up a DT strategy that translates their vision and their ambition for the bank. Leaders should then maintain the strategic direction they've developed while giving themselves the flexibility to adjust the DT plans as needed, achieving a balance through the process between change, quick wins, and legacy, as argued by Peter Dahlström and his McKinsey colleagues in their article, "The seven decisions that matter in a DT: a CEO's guide to reinvention".

in some cases, leaders may join the organization with a DT strategy already in place. If possible, these leaders can adapt the strategy to their vision; if not, they should embrace the strategy. (This situation occurred with several of the panellists – one more reason I recommend short-term DT plans.)

When promoting DT, leaders need to sell their vision through clear communication. They must think carefully about content and channels: what to communicate and when, to whom, and in which format. They cannot limit themselves to one channel or format.

They should also tell a story that gives meaning and sense to the DT. It's important to adopt a personal approach and personalize the story of the transformation to make it meaningful. "Making the transformation" is the first of four elements of a leader's role as advocated by Carolyn Aiken and Scott Keller in their article, "The CEO's role in leading transformation."

The second of Aiken and Keller's elements is "role-modelling desired mindsets and behaviours." Leaders should also incarnate the transformation they are promoting. Be the first to adapt the change. Take symbolic actions, such as showing up with your digital tablets, or use digital tools. Because employees emulate their leaders, consciously or unconsciously, role-modelling desired mindsets and behaviour is an effect approach to leading change.

Ownership and the personal involvement of the CEO throughout the transformation is vital to the success of DT. It's not enough to create the strategy or even to promote it. CEOs need to be fully present and involved for its execution. Like the banks they lead, CEOs need to:

Think Digital for the DT strategy.
Speak Digital for its promotion.
Act Digital in its execution.

Delegation and empowerment might be typically viewed as indications of positive leadership. Not in this case. CEOs cannot delegate the leadership of DT. They need to lead the charge. They need to rally the whole organization, to focus their energy on being relentless engines of change – even intervening to resolve operational issues. "Relentlessly pursuing impact" is the fourth of Aiken and Keller's four elements of a leader's role in a transformation (following "building a strong commitment top team").

In "The seven decisions that matter in a DT," Dahlström and his colleagues summarized the role of the DT leader: Leaders have to make bold decisions about "where business should go, who will lead the effort, how to sell the vision, where to position the firm, how to decide during DT, how to allocate funds, and what to do when."

Naturally, the most energetic of leaders cannot do everything by themselves. Leaders should surround themselves with dedicated leadership teams of senior leaders. The ideal DT team shares the same vision and commitment to DT as the CEO. Membership on this team is not viewed as another task, but as a mission.

How knowledgeable do DT leaders need to be? There is a difference between digital technologies and digital capabilities. Leaders don't need to know how to program, but they do need to know how to speak the new digital language. That is, they need to understand what digital can do and how it works. Henry Mintzberg's metaphor of an orchestra conductor helps explain the difference. A conductor is not a master of all the instruments. Playing the instruments is up to the musicians. The conductor has a vision for the piece and ensures that each musician does what is necessary, including working with the other musicians, to bring that vision alive.

Finally, leaders have the power to make DT fun. As noted above, the more leaders are implicated in DT, the more fun and passion they will find in the process. If the leader finds fun and passion in the transformation, that fun and passion will reflect on employees. I've noted earlier that banks need to elevate the client experience to the point that clients are excited and delighted with the experience. I believe banks need to treat employees the way they treat their clients: helping employees to find the DT experience "delightful." Leaders can do so by putting fun in the process.

Here's another reason to recommend that leaders become fully implicated in DT: to generate fun and passion for employees and even clients – and for themselves. I recommend that leaders enjoy DT, as this will generate success – a virtuous circle!

Chapter Six

Leadership Traits for Conducting DT

This chapter explores theme 5 of the book: *the leadership traits for digital transformation.* The mystique and aura of leaders of the past, much of it coming from exclusive access to information, is gone. Today, everyone in the organization has access to information – about products, market figures, and competitors, for example – once reserved for the bosses. As a result, command-and-control leadership – in which followers obeyed the leader no questions asked – won't work. The leaders are thus developing new leadership styles and leadership traits to replace the lost power and mystique that disappeared with the democratization of information. In chapter 6, I focus on leadership *traits*, while in chapter 7 I will focus on leadership *styles.*

PART 1: ANALYSIS

THREE LEADERSHIP TRAITS

COMMON TO SUCCESSFUL DT LEADERS

From the interviews with the panellists, reinforced by my own observations of DT, three traits emerged as essential for a successful DT.

Optimistic and Innovative Vision

The leaders in the panel were unanimous that a leader must be able to develop and communicate a clear vision of what the bank will become when the transformation is completed – a vision that is both optimistic and innovative about the capabilities of digital and the capabilities of the organization. An *optimistic* vision is not excessively positive: a successful DT strategy is not built on exaggerated hopes. An *innovative* vision pushes the CEO and the organization as a whole to think outside the box. Two examples from the panellists illustrate the importance of vision. In one case, a leader with a clear vision successfully transformed his bank from a small corporate bank to a highly successful digital company worth several times its original value. In contrast, another leader, with no vision of the future bank, relied on bottom-up DT initiatives from the staff to work their way up to top leaders and to the bank's strategy. The inevitable result was significant investment loss in unsuccessful initiatives.

Conviction and Courage

A second trait I observed in successful leaders in the panel was a steadfast conviction in the vital importance of DT, and the courage to carry out and convey this conviction to stakeholders. Courageous leaders were able to persuade shareholders to make a significant investment in DT and in restructuring the organization in unfamiliar ways (creating Agile's "tribes and squads" for example). Several CEOs in the panel convinced their shareholders to invest in DT after putting their jobs on the line: if DT failed, they would resign. Another leader said he would resign immediately if shareholders did not invest in his DT plan. Armed with courage and conviction, these leaders are not afraid to take calculated risks. Nor are they afraid of imperfections or mistakes – either their own or the mistakes of others. They are humble enough to admit when they make mistakes and learn from them: conviction does not mean hubris or an inflated ego.

Ability

The leaders in the panel all have abilities that put them in their positions of leadership. Focusing specifically on abilities relating to DT, I found that successful transformation leaders had the capability to learn and to understand, enabling them to acquire a holistic understanding of the transformation unmatched in the organization with a sufficient level of detail.

This ability to learn did not come without effort: the CEOs took courses and immersed themselves in the transformation, continuously learning about it and from it. The goal was not to merely increase their own individual learning, but to be able to combine their personal knowledge with the knowledge of other DT players and stakeholders to create a comprehensive, useful pool of knowledge that guided the execution of the roadmap.

Successful leaders were also able to execute the transformation, which required a delicate balance of keeping the programme moving forward at a good pace but without taking full control and micro-managing the process. On the one hand, leaders paid attention to the details and had the knowledge to monitor the implementation of the execution plan. They made quick decisions and resolved issues as necessary. On the other hand, they empowered people to do their jobs, making them accountable and responsible. CEOs in the panel emphasized the importance of maintaining this hands-on/hands-off balance. At the same time, in describing the execution of their DT, they clearly understood the details, including the technical aspects of the plan – as opposed to offering the type of vague PR explanations one finds in corporate communications.

PART 2: FINDINGS

SUMMARY OF FINDINGS

Finding 1. A leader must have an optimistic and innovative vision that offers a clear picture of the outcome. "Optimistic and innovative" translates into an ambitious vision, not one that is unrealistic. This vision guides the development of a strategic plan for DT and its execution.

Finding 2. A leader must have the courage to carry his or her conviction, challenging shareholders and employees to embark on an ambitious DT journey that will challenge their comfort zones. A sign of their courage: leaders are ready to assume the risks if the transformation fails – some even putting their jobs explicitly on the line.

Finding 3. A leader needs to be able to understand DT, both holistically in terms of impact on the whole organization and in more detail. Successful leaders are able to immerse themselves in the transformation, continuously learning about it and from it. Finally, leaders have the knowledge and skills to execute the plan, balancing between motivating a timely execution while empowering employees to take on responsibility.

PART 3: DISCUSSION AND RECOMMENDATIONS

Before I begin putting the results of my research in the context of leadership research, it's important to emphasize that during the analysis of the interviews with the panellists, I consciously avoided looking for links to leadership research, letting instead the traits emerge naturally from the descriptions of their experiences.

The greatest scholars and researchers in leadership, starting with Mary Parker Follett, have consistently named **vision** as one of the key characteristics of successful leaders. Vision is a characteristic found consistently in leadership theories. Warren Bennis, for example, defined Leadership as "the capacity to translate vision into reality." A compelling vision is part of Bennis' *Management of Attention*, the first of four competencies of great leaders (the others being Management of Meaning, Management of Trust, and Management of Self).

Research centred specifically on digital leadership and on Agile has also emphasized vision as a key trait. In an IMD report titled, "Redefining Leadership for a Digital Age," Rainer Neubauer and his co-authors cite vision as one of the four HAVE competencies (Humble, Adaptable, Visionary, Engaged) of Agile leaders. "Visionary leaders have a clear sense of long-term direction, even in the face of short-term uncertainty," they write.

Having argued earlier that DT strategy should reflect the leader's vision, I consider vision to be a vital leadership trait to ensure any successful change, but DT in particular. In addition, this vision needs to be optimistic about finding solutions to problems and innovative in the use of digital capabilities. Such a vision can effectively anticipate future threats, find new markets, and develop the viable business model of the future bank. DT begins with developing a strategy, and the leader's vision is at the core of that strategy.

Courage is not as omnipresent in leadership research as vision, although it is cited by many scholars as important. Max Weber notes that without courage, leadership will not embrace the irrationality and deviance needed for creativity and innovation. Bennis would agree, arguing that the path to leadership requires a bit of deviance, audacity, and courage. Pierre Nanterme, the former CEO and Chairman of Accenture who transformed his company with a turn toward new digital services said courage was essential in today's digital era, noting that "being prepared to jump into the new, prepared to lead in volatility and ambiguity, are the traits of the new leaders,"

Just as vision is essential to creating a strategy for DT, courage is essential to execute that strategy. The strategy, after all, is bound to come under fire from shareholders concerned about resources, regulators concerned about new idiosyncratic organizational structures, and clients and employees dealing with new ways of interacting with the bank. Leaders must have the courage to defend their strategy and the vision behind it against all attacks. In addition, the leader needs the courage to shoulder the burden of difficult decisions and potential risks that invariably arise during DT.

Ability as a major characteristic appears in much of the leadership research I reviewed. In their article titled, "Leadership: Do Traits Matter?", Shelley Kirkpatrick and Edwin Locke cite cognitive ability is one of the six traits that distinguish a leader (along with drive, leadership motivation, honesty/integrity, self-confidence, and knowledge of business). Essec's Maurice Thevenet declares that "Leadership is the ability to drive and accomplish a collective action." And Nigel Nicholson a specialist in evolution psychology at the London Business School, considers ability as one of the three core elements of leadership, the others being drive and constitution. Nicholson believes that leaders must be competent in their domains, and smart enough to have a coherent vision. Interestingly, he warns that leaders cannot be too smart or extremely technical if they want to effectively connect with people – who prefer simple and clear to complex.

Ability is therefore a crucial trait for the DT leader. To lead DT, leaders must be able to learn and understand DT, to listen, and to orchestrate and lead this massive endeavour. In terms of specific phases of the project, they must be able to set up a strategy, lead by example to promote the strategy, and follow through to ensure its execution. One final ability might be overlooked: the ability to be humble. Successful DT leaders have the humility to accept mistakes, and to fill gaps of knowledge and skills if necessary.

Vision, courage, and ability may seem to be leadership traits that apply to any situation. These traits, however, are especially required in the context of DT because of the continuous and exponential advance in digital technologies on the one hand and the level of disruption involved on the other: businesses and business models are challenged and often disappear or lose value, and the bank faces additional threats from emerging players in the industry, not to mention new customer and employee behaviour.

I also identified other traits needed for DT:

- **Charisma.** Charisma is especially important during the promotion of DT, when the leader is convincing stakeholders, including shareholders and employees, to buy into the transformation.
- **Proactivity.** To anticipate threats, leaders need to be proactive. Changing the organizational structure to Agile at Scale is one example of this proactivity.
- **Openness and adaptability.** In a VUCA (Volatile, Uncertain, Complex and Ambiguous) world, openness and adaptability are keys to survival. The willingness of leaders in the panel to change their business models and managerial habits exemplifies this openness and adaptability. In one of his last articles, titled "Leadership in a digital world: embracing transparency and adaptive capacity," Bennis emphasized adaptability as the most important attribute for leaders of the digital age. This 'adaptive capacity' included resilience to adversity, openness to the new, being able to learn from failures, and an optimistic sense of can do and can try.

Chapter Seven

Leadership Styles
for Conducting DT

Theme 6 of the book is *the leader's style for digital transformation.* The most important success factor in leading DT is the People, who must be effectively led, motivated, trusted and empowered. As a result, the threats to people that rise up – including job loss or potential job loss; wholesale transformation of jobs; and dramatically new ways of working and interacting with clients and colleagues or managers – present a significant challenge. While in agreement that, as one leader explained, "It is all about the people and our culture," the panellists disagree on which leadership style is best suited to face the challenges of DT.

PART 1: ANALYSIS
WHICH LEADERSHIP STYLE
IS MOST EFFECTIVE?

In the first section of this chapter, I examine several styles highlighted by the panellists, either through their answers to the survey or through my knowledge of their circumstances and history.

The participative or collective style

Many CEOs in the panel approach DT as a collective effort requiring the participation of everyone. A CEO with a background in professional sports compared transformation to a 'group sport.' CEOs who operated with this style of leadership never spoke of 'I', only "we".

Participative leaders are not attempting to pass on responsibility. Instead, they are intent on embarking every employee into the DT effort, enabling the bank to be faster and more flexible and proactive. One CEO, for example, set up a steering committee with members from every hierarchical rank and function in the organization. Another CEO was even bolder, setting up 'Shadow Executive Committees' of young people whose mandate was to challenge Executive Committee decisions.

The directive style

Some CEOs in the panel have a more directive style of leadership that draws on the aura and presence of traditional leaders. Directive leaders are more results-driven than participative leaders: participative words such as 'we', 'trust' and 'values' are replaced by directive words such as 'excellence', 'decision' and 'accelerate'. Directive leaders also embrace top-down Leadership, ready to make unilateral decisions and take the risks that come with responsibility. As one CEO explained, "You have to make decisions, you are paid to make decisions."

Adaptability and contingency

While personality might forge much of a leader's style, situation and context also play a part. In my experience confirmed by the CEOs in the panel, the best leaders adapt their style to the situation. For example, a CEO who tends to be a participative leader will switch to more top-down directive leadership when required.

For long-term DT programmes, many leaders adopted a participative style, which caused some delays in the transformation. However, the participative style also raises the commitment and buy-in of employees. As a result, the participative style may be best suited for larger organizations, where transformation speed is less likely anyway. In addition, with its focus on people and their well-being, participative leadership fits the corporate social responsibility values of many banks.

In general, I found that the banks in the panel who were most advanced on short-term DT were led by more directive leaders. The pace and pressure of the transformation in these banks were clearly more intense than in banks with participative leaders. The focus in these banks was on high performance, disruption, and fast execution and delivery of DT. Talented people with high educational backgrounds thrived in an environment that required them to quickly acquire digital competencies. For others, however, even digital upskilling efforts were not sufficient to help them cope with the pace of transformation and change.

Not all leaders have a single dominant leadership style. Many a leader in the panel combined the participative and directive styles, choosing a 'progressive disruption' DT strategy in which they balanced running the business and disrupting it. These CEOs were also 'adaptable,' favouring one style over the other depending on the circumstances of the moment.

The applied leadership style often depended on the stage of the DT's progress. For example, in the design phase of the DT strategy, most CEOs tended toward the more participative style, bringing in their teams in the brainstorming and design process. The planned length of DT still tempered this participative tendency, as leaders with short-term strategies were less participative than leaders with long-term strategies.

The execution phase was reversed. Here, most CEOs tended towards the more directive leadership style in an effort to advance quickly – although the directive style of participative leaders working on longer-term strategies was still more flexible than the directive style of directive leaders working on short-term strategies.

'Agile at Scale' DT strategies favoured a more participative approach since employee empowerment is built into the process. The leadership focus here was understanding how to orchestrate and monitor the empowered employee, making them accountable for the results expected of them.

For many CEOs, DT sparked a dramatic change in their managerial habits and leadership styles. They had to adapt to new ways of working, new organizational structures, and new managerial practices. Despite the significant change, CEOs were able to adapt and embrace the new practices. Overall, they achieved a balance between total centralized decision-making in which the CEO takes on all decisions and risks, and total decentralized decision-making that allows everyone to make their own decisions – a situation in which everyone is responsible and therefore, in truth, no one is responsible!

PART 2: FINDINGS

SUMMARY OF FINDINGS

For successful DT, CEOs adopt different leadership styles based on context.

Finding 1. Participative leaders want to engage as many people in the effort as possible, while still assuming responsibility for the results.

Finding 2. Directive leaders are focused on performance and execution of the mission. They make the decisions and assume full responsibility.

Finding 3. Leaders adapt their leadership style to the context or situation. Short-term DT strategies were successfully implemented by directive leaders. Longer-term DT strategies were led by participative leaders, although DT was less advanced in their banks.

PART 3: DISCUSSION AND RECOMMENDATIONS

The literature on leadership is filled with references to *participative* leadership. Follet once again leads the way, arguing that leadership implies the participation of people and shared responsibilities at all levels of an organization. Kurt Lewin, the pioneering social psychologist, explored three different leadership styles – the authoritarian (or autocratic) style, the democratic (or participative) style, and the laissez-faire (or delegative) style – and concluded that the participative style of leadership was the best model of leadership for organizations, although it required management skills, trust, and time to put in place. While Rensis Likert (known for the

Likert scale for surveys, with responses ranging from Strongly Agree to Strongly Disagree) favours what he calls the 'non-commanding'style of leadership. He warns that a certain level of maturity, creativity, and competence in the people with whom the leadership is shared is required.

I believe the participative leadership style should be considered by DT leaders, as it increases collaboration and commitment and draws on the knowledge of people in the organization, leading to greater innovation. The participative style will also increase the sense of belonging and engagement of employees – especially the more talented and higher performing employees who want to be part of a bigger success story. This sense of belonging and engagement is evident in the small, specialized teams featured in Agile Management and in which everyone contributes to success.

I do agree with Likert that employees need to demonstrate maturity, creativity, competence, and performance in order for participative leadership to work.

Past research on the *directive* style has noted its strengths, but also its flaws. Several researchers in DT favour the directive style of leadership, including Vivier and Ducrey who, as I have noted, compare DT leadership to that of generals. Likert, in contrast, is an unequivocal opponent of what he calls Exploitative Authoritative Leadership.

In his seminal book, *Economy and Society*, published posthumously, Max Weber's work on authority and legitimacy laid the groundwork for three leadership theories: "Legal Leadership," based on rational authority; "Traditional Leadership" based on the respect for traditions, and "Charismatic Leadership," based on the personality of leaders who are able to inspire devoted followers. Weber favoured legal leadership, grounded in a steadfast "belief in the legality of enacted rules and the right of those elevated to authority under such rules to issue commands." For Weber, Leadership based on rational authority was the basic pillar of efficient and productive organization – although he emphasizes the importance of ethics.

The same nuanced support of directive leadership is presented in the famous Leadership Grid by Robert Blake and Jane Mouton, in which they oppose two major management concerns: concern for people, placed on the y-axis, and concern for production, placed on the x-axis. Thus, the low-on-people, low-on-production 'Impoverished Management', for example, shows up at the lower left part of the grid. In contrast, the high-on-people, high-on-production 'Team Management' is at the upper right portion of the grid (see Figure 9 below). The directive 'Authority/ Obedience Management' is focused exclusively on production while reducing costs and resources. The needs of people are ignored. The result is frustration and tension within the organization. However, in certain situations of crisis in which people could be replaced, Authority/Obedience Management might be appropriate.

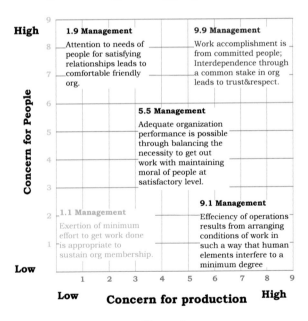

Figure 9.
Blake & Mouton Managerial Grid

I believe CEOs should consider the directive leadership style for DT in certain contexts, notably in short-term DT that requires fast execution and high efficiency. It is important to add that "directive" does not mean "authoritative". Directive leadership is about making the big decisions and accepting responsibility for the outcome of the transformation – and is effective when it incorporates empathy.

In addition to participative and directive leadership, other leadership styles might be considered. Transformation leadership, based on values and meaning (as opposed to transactional leadership) and change leadership based on developing an environment and mindset for changes, are other leadership styles worth considering. In their 1973 HBR article, 'How to choose a leadership pattern,' Robert Tannenbaum and Warren H. Schmidt offer an interesting continuum approach to the debate of 'democratic'vs. 'autocratic' leadership, recognizing that the choice of leadership style is more fluid than style categories might allow for.

Context is an important theme in leadership research. In their book, *Key Concepts in Leadership,* Jonathan Gosling and his co-authors summarize the consensus: "The style to be used is contingent upon such factors as the people, the place, the time, the task, the organization, and other environmental variables."

The choice of leadership styles needs to take into account contextual factors. In this book, I recommend a shorter DT timeframe, when possible, which requires a more directive, non-authoritative, empathy-imbued leadership style that can deliver a fast and successful DT. If a longer timeframe is required, however, I would recommend the participative leadership style, which will keep people focused and committed during the long process.

These combinations of style and timeframe – directive for the shorter timeframe, participative for the longer timeframe – will result in maximum concern for production together with maximum concern for people – that is, they will be located on Blake and Mouton's grid (see page 112) in the most optimal top right corner of the grid, earning a 9,9.

In the end, *the best leadership style is the leader's own*, adapted to the situation, and avoiding the extremes – both extremes of authority but also extremes of empathy and participation.

Chapter Eight

Is DT Leadership Different from "Regular" Leadership?

The final theme of this book is the overall topic of the *leadership of digital transformation.* One might argue that the leadership styles and traits discussed in the previous chapters are general. In this chapter, I explore the question of whether DT requires a specific form of leadership tailored to DT as opposed to what one might call 'regular' leadership. I include the perspective of the panellists on how they are 'living' the DT experience, which gives us further insight into the success factors of DT leadership.

PART 1: ANALYSIS
DT LEADERS VS. 'REGULAR' LEADERSHIP

Is there a specific Leadership required for DT? Is adaptable leadership enough to address the challenges of DT? What is the profile of the successful CEO today and in the future who can lead a transformation? The opinions and practices of the CEOs in the panel diverged on these important questions.

For a few, DT not only requires a new form of leadership, but also new people in leadership positions – especially if CEOs have been in a place for a longer period of time. These CEOs are most likely engrained in the old ways of doing things and will be reluctant to embrace the new digital culture. They may see the CEO role as a representational function, e.g., meeting officials and important clients – a role vastly different from the hands-on role of the DT leader, who understands innovation and is prepared to interact with a new ecosystem of start-ups, innovators, and millennials.

Other leaders in the panel focus on the leadership style, which they say needs to be more directive than in the past. Strong in-command leaders such as Steve Jobs and Jeff Bezos are the prototypes of the DT leader, according to these panellists. As one CEO explains: "Digital imposes a strong management, a strong leader, capable of driving the company in a specific direction."

Other CEOs, however, believe that DT is just another major challenge, another issue that leaders in banking must address and manage. When the global financial crisis started, bank CEOs faced extraordinary challenges and risks that required extraordinary leadership. Despite the stakes involved, CEOs were not expected to transform their leadership styles and approach. So why should dealing with DT be any different, these panellists ask? Leading banks requires a series of competencies to address the regulations, controls, risks, and other issues that financial industry CEOs must face; those competencies will also enable them to deal with DT.

In sum, whether or not DT requires a different kind of leadership is a question on which the panellists diverged. Some believed DT was another change initiative that did not require changes in one's approach to leadership. Many believed DT required a clear understanding of digital technology and digital-related innovation, as well as the strength to make decisions and assume responsibility in times of substantial disruption. For them, the leadership traits and styles of 'regular leadership' had to be questioned.

Living the DT experience

In this section, the CEOs in the panel describe the knowledge required to lead DT, and the personal fun and excitement they find in the challenge.

Digital technology knowledge

How important is digital knowledge to DT leaders? Leaders don't have to master new technologies, but they do have to understand technologies and their capabilities – which requires a certain base of technological knowledge. They recommend starting with general, less complicated knowledge (how data is organized, what is Robotics Process Automation...) to the more sophisticated, such as understanding Blockchain, APIs, and Artificial

Intelligence. Understanding digital technologies in this way will help CEOs better understand and evaluate innovations in the marketplace – for example, the new offerings from start-ups or Fin-Techs that could challenge the bank's business model, or, as we saw earlier, disrupt the bank's value chain.

Having an IT background or technological skills will give certain CEOs a head start. Those who don't have such a background will need to invest in self-learning about technologies if they are to succeed. Most CEOs in the panel had specialized training in digital technologies in preparation of a DT in their banks. Some went further with immersion seminars – some involving weeks at specialized technology and innovation centres to fully understand the technology and its possibilities. These seminars did not involve the CEO alone; other members of the top management team also participated, a reflection of how DT involves every corner of the bank. The return on time and cost of immersion training is high since the knowledge equips CEOs and their management teams to set the priorities and make the decisions, as one immersion veteran explains: It is important to know where to put your scarce resources in terms of investments but also in terms of talent, and to do that you have to identify how useful the innovation is for the client, for the bank, but most importantly how much will it generate business.

One overriding insigh emerges from the discussion with the panellists: while fundamental leadership and management skills are essential, CEOs who want to succeed as DT leaders need to love or learn to love technology. They need to be enthusiastic about adopting technology rather than rejecting it. Those who do not fully understand and appreciate the capabilities of technologies are not likely to successfully lead DT.

Which leads to another surprisingly important facet of DT leadership: the fun factor.

The Fun factor

Beautiful, Fun, Challenging, Exciting, Positive, Magnificent Experience, Enjoying it... It's clear from the words that the panellists use when describe how they are living DT: These CEOs are having fun! Not all, of course. Some CEOs are more "strategists" than "owners" of the transformation – that is, they are less directly involved and committed to DT. These CEOs might recognize that DT is exciting, but don't particularly find it amusing. Other arm's-length CEOs are serene, confident in their team's efforts to get the job done. Still others would be more enthusiastic about DT if only they had the time.

For most CEOs in the panel, however, DT is an exciting and enjoyable undertaking. What I call the "fun factor" is linked to the level of involvement: the more a CEO is implicated in the DT, the higher the fun factor. For some, it's working with top people with different backgrounds. For others, it's the joy of learning.

Some CEOs enjoy the overlap, or "porosity", between their professional and personal lives; these CEOs are happy to see that banking, in the form of online banking and other digital functions, has joined the daily digital activities (e.g., online shopping, music apps) that are now an integral part of our daily lives.

Other CEOs in the panel were excited by the sheer breadth and import of the technological change. As one CEO explains: "DT fascinates me because it's an exceptional change, it's like the invention of electricity." This CEO, as did many others, recognized the complexity of the challenge involved, but it was this complexity that made the project even more exciting.

The joy of working on something so complex and challenging was reflected in other comments. "It is very time consuming, but very rewarding, especially when you see that it works and you get people behind you," says one CEO. And as for the inevitable setbacks and failures, well, dealing with them is part of the job of a leader. As one

CEO says, "The role of the CEO is to manage through the storm."

These examples reveal the link between the fun factor and the personal character of the CEOs. These leaders enjoy challenges. They enjoy complex undertakings. Some of the panellists admit that they get bored easily, and DT is never boring. As one CEO explains, "For me it's great, there's always something to do, there's always something to work on."

PART 2: FINDINGS
SUMMARY OF FINDINGS
In this section, I bring in some findings from the previous chapters on leadership to present an overview on leadership in general.

Finding 1. In the digital age, leaders can no longer draw their authority and control from the aura or mystique of being the leader, or from their monopolistic access to information. They need to find new ways of leading that fit the requirements of the digital era.

Finding 2. Leading DT will give leaders the opportunity to experience additional satisfaction and success as leaders. Many leaders, especially those fully implicated in DT, find the challenge fun and exciting. Porosity, the alignment between personal and professional lives and activities, adds to the excitement.

Finding 3. Some leaders believe DT is just another challenge and responsibility for CEOs. Most, however, believe that leading DT requires a specific type of leadership, one that includes a willingness to acquire an understanding of digital capabilities, and is strong enough to lead people into the substantial change.

Finding 4. The most important success factor in leading DT, as in leading organizations in general, is People – specifically the ability to motivate, trust, and accompany them through the transformation.

PART 3: DISCUSSION AND RECOMMENDATIONS

Leadership is key to any large change initiative, and is even more important for DT, when information and knowledge are accessible to everyone. The transparency of the digital age requires leaders to step up and take responsibility for their decisions.

As shown in the previous chapters on leadership, DT leaders might have different styles and traits. They can only have one mindset, however, and that is the mindset of an innovator and disruptor. Banks have a choice: to be the disruptor or to be disrupted. Leaders must take the responsibility to ensure their banks are the disruptors.

Activating this mindset requires, as Vivier and Ducrey note in their *Guide for DT*, 'culling of the sacred cow' – that is, getting rid of bad habits and obsolete processes, no matter how important they might have been in the past.

Therefore, my recommendation is that CEOs be prepared to embrace the digital culture and learn the new 'code' for leading in the digital era. Only then can they maintain the strong leadership required – but a strength that is different from leadership strength of the past based on command and control. Strong leadership today must have empathy at its core.

Shahyan Khan identified three leadership forms in the modern era:

Values-based Leadership, based on integrity, trust, listening and respect of followers.

Transformation Leadership, based on idealized influence, inspiration motivation, intellectual stimulation, and individualized consideration.

Authentic Leadership, based on self-awareness, relational transparency, balanced processing, and internalized moral perspective. For Kahn, digital tools and practices enhances what he calls the 'virtual presence' of leaders and increases their 'holistic approach' with internal and external components of the digital ecosystem.

In sum, an interesting two-way dynamic exists between leadership and DT success. Leadership impacts the success of DT, but DT success in turn impacts leadership success. Leading a successful DT enhances the leadership capabilities of the CEO by demystifying leadership and making it more efficient, accessible, and involved. DT success can thus impact the careers of CEOs.

Leading DT requires a strong, knowledgeable, and holistic leadership that change initiatives of the past did not require. DT is not just another action item or initiative on the leader's checklist. It is a mission, and it will set the stage for other missions in the future (or even in the present), such as Corporate Social Responsibility and Sustainable Finance.

In the way that all roads lead to Rome, all the research, analysis and discussion described in the chapters on leadership indicate that leading DT is first and foremost about people. Or, to put it another way, concerns about people drive the leadership decisions of a DT leader.

Understanding digital capabilities, for example, is essential to be able to communicate with the technology professionals and others in the digital ecosystem, and to more effectively communicate the purpose and processes of the transformation to managers, employees, and other internal stakeholders. I've emphasized the importance of strong leadership with *empathy*, to further strengthen the leader's connection with people.

Leadership theorists going back to Mary Parker Follett have talked of the importance of the central role of people. For Warren Bennis, for example, trust and empowerment are two of the four essential competencies of a leader (the other two being the management of attention and meaning). (See Table 1 below)

Management of Attention	*Ability to draw others to them.* *Focus on Commitment.* *Compelling vision.*
Management of Meaning	*Make dreams apparent to others and align people with them.* *Make ideas tangible.* *Create meaning.*
Management of Trust	*Trust is essential to all organizations.* *Need for reliability.* *Need for constancy.*
Management of Self	*Knowing one's skills.* *Nurture their strengths.* *Be well acquainted with the concept of failure.*
Empowerment: ***The Effects of Leadership***	*Real Leadership can be felt through an organization. Empowerment is the collective effect of Leadership:* *1- People feel significant. Everyone feels that he or she makes difference to the organization.* *2- Learning and competence matter. Leaders value learning and mastery, and so do people who work for leaders.* *3- People feel part of a community. Where there is Leadership, there is a team, a family, a unity.* *4- Work is exciting. Where there are leaders, work is stimulating, challenging, fascinating and fun.*

Table 1.
Four Competencies of Great Leaders.
(Source: Bennis, W, 1987)]

Obsessing about people is in my view as vital as obsessing about innovation, successful DT leaders in the panel maintained their intense focus on people during the transformation.

Inevitably, you might have some employees who cannot adjust to the changes brought by DT – employees who may even leave the bank. Many employees, however, will become fully implicated in the transformation. (Ironically, the pace of the transformation can play a role in the engagement of employees, who may start to drift away if the process is too slow.)

In sum, people should be the major preoccupation and focus of the leader.

One final note: trust, engagement, and empathy are reciprocal attributes. Leaders who trust, are engaged with, and show empathy to their people will receive trust, engagement, and empathy in return, which is key to the success of DT: No CEO can do it alone, and everyone in the organization needs to contribute.

Chapter Nine

Conclusion: The CEO's Guide for a Successful Digital Transformation

The previous seven chapters combined the results of my research with the bank leaders in our panel with my personal knowledge and experience of digital transformation – including personal knowledge of a number of DTs in the panel – and literature on leadership and DT. Analysing the gathered information and knowledge from these three sources led to the identification of the seven themes that anchored the previous chapters. Each chapter ended with recommendations for DT leaders.

In this chapter, I synthesize these recommendations to create a CEO's guide for successful DT consisting of five managerial recommendations detailed below. Although these recommendations are based on research with banks, they apply to all companies, regardless of sector.

1. DT is a substitution, not a complement

The transformation is not an additional feature or item to add to the company's offerings. Nor is it another project or another initiative among many projects or initiatives. DT does not complement what the company is currently doing or what it currently offers. Instead, almost everything needs to be substituted or digitalized. All products and services need to be conceived, created, and provided digitally. Services that require human interaction and empathy will continue to be offered but will be aided or enhanced digitally as much as possible.

In order to achieve this wholesale substitution, the leader must understand the core elements of what will be transformed, that is customer experience, employee experience, and business model.

- Companies need to invest more on customer experience, notably in an effort to generate emotions and delight, as opposed to focusing on customer interactions. Every customer will benefit from digital, including high net worth individuals working with private bankers. To believe that they don't require digital is a dangerous myth.

- The entire value chain of the company needs to be digitalized, from the front office, client-facing interactions to all back-office processes, which will not only enhance operational efficiency but transform the employee experience. Both employees and clients want a certain porosity between their experiences in their daily lives and their experiences with companies either as employees or clients. For example, they want to take care of their online banking needs in the same way that they can take care of renting a hotel room or buying a book online.

- Companies need to reconsider and redefine their value chains, which are at risk of being disrupted and even broken apart. Following the 'if you can't beat them join them' mindset, financial services companies should become a platform for providing financial services, and partner with, or even invest in, players in the new digital ecosystem such as FinTechs and neo banks.

It's inevitable that some jobs will disappear with DT, but others will be created. DT will offer employees opportunities, but these employees need to be upskilled by their companies, that is provided with specific training to acquire the new digital skills they need to continue to be value-adding employees.

2. A successful DT strategy is a top-down strategy

The first step in the digital journey is for the CEO to develop the strategy for the organization – a strategy that reflects the holistic perspective of the CEO, and includes a plan for prioritizing investments and allocating resources to digitalize everything when possible. And if everything cannot be digitalized, then the plan sets priorities for innovations that are useful, scalable, profitable, efficient, risk reducing, and can be quickly implemented.

This strategy should be driven top-down by the leader. Bottom-up approaches are rarely successful. This top-down strategy encompasses a detailed roadmap focused on the ultimate destination rather than 'as you go' initiatives. Although detailed, the roadmap must remain dynamic, continuously challenged, and able to be adapted.

The destination should not be too far off: shorter transformation time frames – from 18 to 24 months – are more efficient and effective. Longer DT periods run a greater risk of missing the targets and losing the support of clients who would run out of patience.

The timing of DT is also important: companies need to be proactive and anticipate threats no matter how positive the KPIs in the short term. Companies are innovation trend-setters or first followers; they ought to introduce digital services to customers, not the other way around.

Internal and external communication must be prolific through the transformation. Keeping employees informed will help alleviate the fear of change and increase engagement and commitment. Keeping clients informed will reassure them that the company will keep its promises.

In addition to the three major elements of DT – customer experience, operational efficiency, and business model – a DT strategy should also transform the culture and mindset of the organization. This mindset and culture can be summarized as 'Think Digital' (put digital in all processes and activities), 'Act Digital' (translate thinking into action), and 'Speak Digital' (interact digitally with stakeholders and the new digital ecosystem).

Investing in digital technologies begins with investing in the structuring and securitization of data. Companies will need Apps and Application Programming Interfaces (APIs) through which they share the data with clients and the ecosystem. A wide range of other digital technologies – including Cloud Computing, Robotic Process Automation and Artificial Intelligence – will further advance the DT strategy.

3. Agile and Agility, both are the questions... and the answers

'Legacy' represents a major challenge to the success of DT. The legacy of systems, of clients, and of people pulls toward the past and not the future. DT solves the issue of legacy systems with better systems, and the issue of legacy clients with better customer experience. The challenge of legacy people inside the organization is not so easily resolved – and can prove costly to address.

To address the challenge of legacy systems and people, and ensure a successful transformation, I recommend deploying Agile on three levels.

For software development, use 'Agile Methodology', based on people, interactions, and customer collaboration. There may be some times, however, when classic methodologies such as Waterfall are more effective.

For managing the organization, use 'Agile Management', which internally manifests itself through less bureaucracy and more transparency, and externally manifests through collaboration with clients on iterations of products and services.

Finally, for restructuring the organization, use 'Agile at Scale', a complete restructuring that breaks down silos, aligns employees around common objectives, and increases their motivation and engagement. At the heart of an Agile at Scale structure are cross-functional teams with the knowledge to deliver products and projects.

4. DT is not delegable

The role of the CEO in DT unfolds in three incremental steps:

- Strategy: The CEO develops a top-down DT strategy based on his or her vision and ambition for the company, obtains and allocates the necessary resources to different projects and teams, and maintains the strategy dynamic, allowing adjustments as appropriate.

- Promotion. To promote the DT strategy, the CEO incarnates the transformation, personalizing the story of the transformation, and role-modelling the transformation to inspire employees.
- Ownership. The CEO needs to 'own' the transformation by being personally involved and invested in every step, including following up on its execution.

DT is not delegable. It requires bold decisions that the CEO must not be afraid to take. It requires a CEO who leads the charge, laying down the transformation's strategy, promoting the transformation, and owning the transformation.

While taking charge of the transformation, CEOs can't go at it alone. They need dedicated teams who share the CEO's vision and sense of mission.

CEOs don't need to master the digital technologies, but they do need to understand what these technologies can do – just like an orchestra conductor who doesn't need to master every instrument, but does need to be fully aware of their capabilities.

For CEOs fully involved in the process, DT will be fun. This fun factor is a virtuous circle; emanating from the CEO, it revitalizes the employee experience, and enchants the customer.

5. In DT, Leadership is key

Leadership is always critical for organizations, but for leading DT, even more so.

In terms of leadership traits, CEOs need an optimistic and innovative vision that anticipates threats and opportunities. They need courage to put strategy into action and make bold decisions. They need the ability to understand digital capabilities, with the willingness to immerse themselves in digital training if necessary. Finally, they need an open, curious, adaptable mindset to embrace the new.

In terms of leadership style, a more directive leadership style focused on performance can be effective, when tempered with empathy. However, it is the CEOs who can best determine where on the style continuum between participatory and directive styles is the combination that best works for them.

Leaders cannot lean on their aura for their authority. The leader's aura is demystified. CEOs need to rule on the strength of their ability and willingness to step up and assume responsibility. And they should be ready to deploy a disruptive mindset that sweeps through the organization and makes everyone think outside the box. And they too need to think digital, act digital and speak digital to maintain their leadership.

Transformation is about change. DT is about the continuous evolution in technologies. CEOs must be obsessed by the constant disruption of business models, innovations, customer experience, and operational efficiency unleashed by DT. Thus, leadership of DT is a specific leadership, one that is knowledgeable and holistic and recognizes DT as a mission, not just another activity.

Finally, CEOs must be even more obsessed with perhaps the overriding key success factor of DT: people. CEOs must be obsessed with getting the people on board the DT journey, trusting them, and generating empathy for them. A people obsession can only be rewarding for the leader.

Final Remarks

As I wrote in the Note from the Author at the beginning of the book, my goal in publishing the original full research paper *Leadership of Digital Technology* was to present my research on the theory and practice of leading DT in the financial services industry, and to use this research to create practical guidelines for CEOs seeking to plan and implement DT.

This book is intended for all senior executives and board members within the financial sector, be it in banking, insurance, asset management and fund industry, and all other related activities.

The managerial implications that emerged from the research behind this book would prove to be useful to me on a personal and professional level – a clear indication of its practical value for leaders and the reason I wanted to disseminate the research more widely.

My takeaway from the research and lessons in this book – and I hope it is your takeaway as well – is not an attitude that I now know everything. On the contrary, the more I learn, the more I continuously challenge my knowledge and even my leadership.

And this continuous learning and growth makes the process much more enjoyable. I am having fun – and I believe you will, too.

Further Reading

Aiken, C. B., & Keller, S. P. (2007). The CEO's role in leading transformation. *McKinsey Quarterly. Retrieved, 27.*

Bennis, W. (1987). Four competencies of great leaders. *Executive Excellence, 4*, 2-14.

Bennis, W. (2013). Leadership in a digital world: embracing transparency and adaptive capacity. *Mis Quarterly, 37*(2), 635-636.

Bennis, W., & Nanus, B. (1985). The strategies for taking charge. *Leaders, New York: Harper. Row, 41.*

Blake, R. R., & Mouton, J. S. (1981). Management by Grid® principles or situationalism: Which? *Group & Organization Studies, 6*(4), 439-455.

Body, L., & Tallec, C. (2015). *L'expérience client: le design pour innover, l'humain pour créer du lien, le collaboratif pour accompagner le changement.* Éditions Eyrolles.

Caldwell, J. I., & Crippen, C. (2015). The leadership philosophy of Mary Parker Follett (1868- 1933). *The International Journal of Servant-Leadership, 11*(1), 187-227.

Cherry, K. (2006). Leadership styles. *Retrieved from.* Christensen, C. M. (1997). *The Innovator's Dilemma.* Boston: Harvard Business School Press.

Dahlström, P., Desmet, D., & Singer, M. (2017). The seven decisions that matter in a digital transformation: A CEO's guide to reinvention. *Digital McKinsey article (Feb 2017).*

De la Boutetière, H., Montagner, A. & Angelika Reich, A. (2018). Unlocking success in digital transformations. *McKinsey & Company, 1-14.*

Deloitte Center for Financial Services. (2016) *Banking reimagined. How disruptive forces will radically transform the industry in the decade ahead,* Deloitte Development LLC.

Fitzgerald, M., Kruschwitz, N., Bonnet, D., & Welch, M. (2014). Embracing digital technology:

A new strategic imperative. *MIT Sloan Management Review, 55(2), 1.*

Goodman, J. (2014). *Customer experience 3.0: High-profit strategies in the age of techno service.* Amacom.

Gosling, J., Sutherland, I. & Jones, S. (2012). *Key concepts in leadership.* Sage. Grint, K., Jones, O.S., & Holt, C. (2016) What is leadership: Person, Result, Position or Process, or all or None of These? *The Routledge companion to leadership,* 3-20.

Groutel, E., Carluer, F., & Le Vigoureux, F. (2010). Le leadership follettien: un modèle pour demain? *Management Avenir,* (6), 284-297.

Kane, G. C. (2018). Introduction to Marie-Cecile, C. How to Go Digital. Practical Wisdom to Help Drive Your Organization's Digital Transformation. *MIT Sloan Management Review, New York.* 2018 BASED ON 5.2.2. THEME DISCUSSION FIRST PARAGRAPH

Khan, S. (2016). *Leadership in the digital age: A study on the effects of digitalisation on top management leadership.*

Kirkpatrick, S. A., & Locke, E. A. (1991). Leadership: do traits matter? *Academy of management perspectives, 5*(2), 48-60.

Michelman, P. (2016). Leading in an unpredictable world. *MIT Sloan Management Review, 58*(1), 53.

Mintzberg, H. (2009). *Managing.* Pearson Education.

Neubauer, R., Tarling, A., & Wade, M. (2017). *Redefining leadership for a digital age.* Global Center for Digital Business Transformation. CISCO, IMD.

Nicholson, N. (2001). Managing the human animal. *Industrial Management & Data Systems.* Oberer, B., & Erkollar, A. (2018). Leadership 4.0: Digital leaders in the age of industry

4.0. *International Journal of Organizational Leadership.* Pesqueux, Y. (2020). *A propos des théories du leadership.* Thèse de Doctorat. France. halshs- 02524246

Pine, B. J., & Gilmore, J. H. (1999). *The Experience Economy*. Harvard Business School Press, Boston.

Plane, J. M. (2015). *Théories du leadership: modèles classiques et contemporains.* Dunod.

Swedberg, R., & Agevall, O. (2016). *The max weber dictionary: Key words and central concepts* (Second ed.). Stanford Social Sciences, an imprint of Stanford University Press.

Tannenbaum, R., & Schmidt, W. H. (1973). How to choose a leadership pattern. *Harvard Business Review, 51*(3).

Vivier, E., & Ducrey, V. (2019). *Le guide de la transformation digitale.* Eyrolles.

Vogel, P., & Hultin, G. (2018). Introduction: Digitalization and Why Leaders Need to Take It Seriously. In: *Conquering digital overload* (pp. 1-8). Palgrave Macmillan, Cham.

About the Author

Jean ELIA (aka John ELIA) has more than 28 years of experience in the financial sector, including 17 as CEO of major life insurance companies. He started his career working for a UK insurance company, before joining Société Générale Assurances at their subsidiary in Lebanon. He later advised a number of insurance companies in the Middle East and North Africa region before before being appointed as CEO of Société Générale Assurances Subsidiaries in Egypt and Morocco respectively. In 2013 he became CEO of SOGELIFE, a leading life insurance company in Luxembourg providing wealth planning solutions across Europe.